"I Hope You're Living As High on The Hog As The Pig You Turned Out to Be"

"I Hope You're Living As High on The Hog As The Pig You Turned Out to Be"

By Bill Anderson

LONGSTREET PRESS
ATLANTA, GEORGIA

Published by
LONGSTREET PRESS, INC.
A subsidiary of Cox Newspapers,
A division of Cox Enterprises, Inc.
2140 Newmarket Parkway
Suite 118
Marietta, GA 30067

Printed in the United States of America

2nd printing 1994
Library of Congress Catalog Number: 93-79670
ISBN 1-56352-099-0

Jacket design by Laura McDonald
Book design by Laurie Shock
Cover illustration by Mike Lester

This book was printed by R.R. Donnelley & Sons, Harrisonburg, Virginia.
The text was set in Bembo

To all the pickers, singers, songwriters, disc jockeys, promoters and fans who were country long before country was cool.

Also by Bill Anderson

Whisperin' Bill, An Autobiography

And to my mom and dad, Lib and Jim Anderson, who taught me to look for and appreciate the humor in life. And who never once told me to put down my guitar and go get a real job.

*"We're in a fun business.
If you're not having fun,
you're not doing your job right."*

Cowboy Jack Clement

Country music songwriter,

record producer, publisher,

and resident philosopher.

PROLOGUE

The music business is not rocket science. Neither is it brain surgery, nuclear physics, technology by which to end world hunger, nor even Algebra II.

It's entertainment, that's what it is. Pure and simple entertainment. And Jack Clement hit it on the head: Do it right and the business of entertainment is fun.

I must have done it right a few times, because I've had a blast!

I have spent my entire life in one way or another involved with entertainment, in particular with country music. For more than thirty years now I have made my living as a country music disc jockey, songwriter, recording artist, on-stage performer, television personality, music publisher, radio station owner, author, and rhinestone-wearin', guitar-pickin', whisperin' ambassador of fun, frivolity, and song. Like most in the entertainment business, I take my craft seriously. Unlike some, I try not to take *myself* very seriously at all.

I owe everything I have or have ever had to country music: Thousands of quiet, restful, dream-filled nights and one nasty ole sleep-stealing ulcer. Glamorous and exciting trips to far-flung places like London, England; Paris, France; and Stockholm, Sweden. Not-so-glamorous-and-exciting trips to Grundy, Virginia; Jerome, Idaho; and Ottumwa, Iowa. (Ottumwa, by the way, I learned years ago on a frigid, snow-laden night, is an old Indian word meaning "empty auditorium.")

Country music and country music alone has provided me with the opportunity to meet governors, senators, presidents, and Grandpa Jones; with the chance to be rich and famous and almost bankrupt; to fly around the world in jet planes and ride two hundred miles across Canada in a taxicab; to make a whole bunch of friends and one or two enemies; to laugh and cry and feel and hurt and commiserate, and then to stand up, dust myself off, and do it all over again.

When the great music poet Bob McDill wrote in his classic song, "Amanda," that "a measure of people don't understand / the pleasures of life in a hillbilly band," he may well have composed the most understated truth ever set to music.

I have tried for most of my professional life to tell normal people (i.e., those who engage themselves in worthwhile endeavors outside the entertainment business) about my work and the marvelous world in which I have been (and still am) privileged to live, breathe, and participate. Invariably, most normals smile, nod their heads, and look at me through glazed-over eyes that say, "I don't have the foggiest idea what you're talking about."

But I don't give up easily. Ever since the day I laughed at my first "car comedian" telling his first funny road story, I've thought, "Somebody ought to write a book about the pure joy that exists inside this crazy business." That was usually met by, "Aw, nobody'd believe it." Or, "They'd file it under 'fiction' in the public library." Well, maybe they will, but I've decided to take a shot at it anyhow. At least a book will have been composed and filed somewhere. To my way of thinking, that's better than risking that a marvelous slice of Americana—the country music world my friends and I came into and have inhabited for the past thirty-plus years—might be ignored or forgotten, swept away by the winds of time or change, and lost forever.

Collecting, compiling, and laughing at these stories all over again has not necessarily made me want to go back and live the times once more, but in a way it has made me feel strangely warm and smug inside. Sort of like I found the key to a tightly locked door, walked inside a long forgotten room, and was caressed there by the gentle, comforting glow of a candle from a winter's night past. And it has reminded me more than once of my grandmother and what she said to her inquisitive, young grandson one time when I asked her why she devoted one entire upstairs room in her house to nothing but the storing of junk: "Someday, Billy," she smiled, "if we leave that junk up there long enough, it will turn into antiques."

Maybe that's what has happened to me. Maybe I have finally been around this business of country music long enough for the junk in my past to turn antique—for the long, hard days and the endless, empty miles to turn humorous and laughable.

But be forewarned: Title notwithstanding, this is not a joke book. Neither is it a history book nor an anthology. It's not a kiss 'n' tell collection of who has slept with whom, who got drunker than whom, or who within the ranks of country music has popped the most pills, sniffed the most coke, smoked the most grass, cheated on the greatest number of husbands or wives, is or isn't gay, has or hasn't spent time in jail. It is simply the sharing of one person's medley of significant and sometimes insignificant remembrances—some funny, some sad, some poignant—gathered in widely spaced travels along a thirty-year road.

Much of what you are about to read is set not in a time that *is* but comes, rather, from a season that *was*. In some respects, it's a reflection of a way of life that doesn't even exist anymore and may never exist again. But, believe me, it was once very much alive.

In fact, young friends of mine in the country music business today often refer in near reverence to this era as "the golden age of country music." Maybe it was, maybe it wasn't. Perhaps the years have simply turned it golden in everyone's mind.

Mother Nature has somehow endowed most of us with an uncanny ability to forget muddy boots, out-of-tune guitars, and pot-holes in the crooked roads anyhow, and to recall instead warm summer nights, crystal-clear sound systems, and standing ovations—allowing us the luxury of looking over our shoulders at the past through soft-focus lenses and seeing gold where there was, in reality, only bronze. Or was it rust?

Hopefully these pages will help bring it to life again—whatever it was—and will aid in preserving it awhile longer, if for no other reason than to stoke the fires of pleasant remembrance in the hearts and minds of those of us who were fortunate enough to have been there.

"Maybe that wasn't the way it was, but they're my memories and I'll remember them the way I want to."

Jeannie Seely

Grand Ole Opry star

"I Hope You're Living As High on The Hog As The Pig You Turned Out to Be"

CHAPTER ONE

In the beginning, it was us against them.

Not everybody believes that now in these, the salad days of country music, but there was a time in the not-so-distant history of our art form when they thought we were dumb and a bunch of bumpkins. We accused them of being snobs. They said we had no sophistication. We said that was better than having no soul. They turned up their noses and said our music was too simplistic. We reminded them that vanilla outsells all the other flavors of ice cream. And on it went, back and forth, tit for tat, for more years than I care to remember.

Their view of us as something slightly less than first-class citizens was stamped indelibly into my consciousness one morning more than thirty years ago. I can laugh at it now. I'm not sure just how funny I thought it was at the time.

I was standing on the sunswept sidewalk of Eighth Avenue, North, in downtown Nashville, nervously clutching a worn twenty-dollar bill in my left hand, trying hard to remember everything I had been told.

"Whatever you do," Roger Miller had pleaded right up to the last, "don't tell them you're in the music business."

"But I am in the music business," I argued. "What else could I possibly say?"

"Tell 'em you're in the publishing business," Roger offered. "That's no lie. You write songs for Tree Publishing Company. They probably don't know that Tree publishes music. Just say you're in the publishing business. He can do that, can't he Bud?"

Buddy Killen, vice president of Tree Publishing, smiled from behind his boss's shiny mahogany desk and nodded his head. "Sure, help yourself."

"I'm not sure I can lie about it," I said, "but I'll try. Thanks."

I double-checked the address I had been given against the number painted over the door. I was at the right place. I took a deep breath and walked in.

The smiling face of an attractive young lady behind the counter disarmed me immediately. "May I help you?" she asked.

"Yes, ma'am. I'd like to sign up for telephone service," I replied.

"Sure," she smiled. "Have you ever had a telephone in Nashville before?"

"No, ma'am. I've just moved to town."

"Well, fill out this sheet of paper and someone over there will help you." She pointed to several rows of desks behind her where a group of clerks and secretaries all appeared to be hard at work.

I took the application and retreated to a chair by the window. I began filling in the blanks: Name, address, employer, job description. "Don't tell them you're in the music business," I could almost hear Roger saying, as if he were a little bird perched on my shoulder.

"Aw, what the heck?" I thought to myself. "These seem like nice folks.

Tom T. Hall

Eddy Arnold has long been recognized as one of country music's most astute businessmen.

In the late fifties, he went into the real estate business in the then rural community of Brentwood, south of Nashville. Not only did Eddy buy up much of the lush, rolling farmland that would later be sold to housing developers, but he also was the guiding force behind the formation of the Brentwood Water Company.

In later years, many country music stars would move to Brentwood and receive their water from Eddy's company. One of these was Tom T. Hall, who moved into the palatial Fox Hollow estate.

"It really makes me mad," Tom T. said one day, grinning as he spoke. "Every time I flush my toilet, Eddy Arnold makes a nickel!"

What can they do to me if I tell them the truth? Shoot me? Run me out of town?" So I wrote that my employer was Tree Publishing Company and that I was, indeed, in the music business.

I gave Ma Bell the rest of the information she requested and told the smiling young lady who had greeted me that I was ready to move ahead. She scoured the rows of desks in the big office and pointed toward one where an employee seemed to be between tasks. "She'll take care of you," the young lady said, and I stepped behind the counter. I walked confidently to the desk I had been assigned.

"Hello," I said cheerfully to the prim, middle-aged clerk with the wire-rimmed glasses, the plain black dress, no lipstick, and the tightly wrapped bun on the back of her head. I got no response, so I simply handed her my completed application form and helped myself to a seat in a vacant chair alongside her desk. She dutifully took my paper and, without a word, began to scan what I had written.

It seemed like forever before she spoke. "Well, Mr. Anderson, I see you're in the music business," she finally said, raising her eyebrows and smiling ever so slightly.

"Yes, ma'am," I replied proudly, sitting up a little taller in my chair and trying not to sound like I was bragging. I almost added, "I wrote 'City Lights' for Ray Price and I've just signed a recording contract with Decca Records," but I suddenly remembered what Roger and Buddy had told me. I decided to save the heavy artillery for later.

"Well, that will be $100," she announced curtly, not even looking in my direction but swiftly sliding my application off the top of her desk and onto her lap. The next stop, I feared, was about to be the trash can.

"I beg your pardon?" I stammered.

"$100, Mr. Anderson. In order for you to obtain a telephone and be connected for service it will cost you a deposit of $100."

"Nobody said anything about that yesterday when I called," I said defensively. "I was told you only required a deposit of $15. I have that right here." I flashed my $20 bill.

"That's right, Mr. Anderson, if you're not in the music business it is $15. Everyone in the music business, however, pays a $100 deposit. Either that or they don't get a telephone." She seemed to be receiving some sort of perverse

At the taping of the Sixty-fifth anniversary of the Grand Ole Opry television special, the young ladies in the audience began screaming hysterically when young, good-looking Clint Black walked on stage.

Veteran Roy Clark was standing nearby and put the scene into perspective.

"Don't get the big-head, Clint," Roy said with a smile. "Their mamas used to do the same thing for me!"

Bill and Ray Price

joy from watching me squirm. From her looks, I'd have guessed it was probably the most fun she'd had in years.

But I still couldn't believe my ears. $100 for a *deposit* on a phone? I didn't want to buy the company, for goodness sake, I simply wanted a telephone. One black, rotary-dial telephone to sit on a table, with a line from the nearest pole to my little cabin. It sounded simple enough to me.

But I was trapped and I knew it. I stuffed the $20 back into my jeans, reached into my jacket, withdrew my brand-new checkbook from First American Bank, and trying hard to keep my hands from shaking, nervously filled out check number 001 in the amount of $100. I tore it off the top of the pad and handed it to my new-found friend. "Now . . . when do I get this back?" I asked as casually as I could, hoping she couldn't detect the panic in my voice.

"Once you've established sufficient credit with us," she snapped, looking not at all pleased that I had been able to play her little game, yet never suspecting that I had just mortgaged next month's groceries in return for quenching my suddenly insatiable thirst for a telephone. "But you must pay your bills in full and on time," she admonished. "Most people in the music business don't do that. They run up huge long distance bills calling people all over the country, and then when they can't pay, we have to take their phones out. By the way, you don't happen to know where we might find any of these people do you?" She handed me a lengthy list of typewritten names. I recognized three or four of them—a couple of booking agents, a guitar player, a singer I hadn't heard of in years—but I didn't volunteer any information. I assumed they were people who hadn't paid their phone bills and I wasn't about to rat on them. Especially to Miss Sunshine. "I guess you might come down to the Opry some Saturday night," I said non-chalantly. "Some of 'em probably hang out down there."

She didn't say a word, but the look on her face told me she'd rather split a pint of Mad Dog 20/20 with the winos inside the men's room at the bus station than to go in search of phone bill dodgers at the Ryman Auditorium and the Grand Ole Opry.

"That will be all, Mr. Anderson," she announced tersely, reaching out and retrieving her paper from my grasp. I had an urge to bite her on the leg.

Songstress Becky Hobbs received the following letter from a fan in Kansas City who had recently been to Nashville:

"Dear Becky:

I had such a good time at Fan Fair this year. I had to stand in line an hour just to get to see Garth Brooks and hug him and get his autograph. Then I stood in another long line to see Randy Travis. While I was standing there, I saw a man in line ahead of me who looked like Garth only a little taller and older and just for a moment, when his eyes met mine, I really wished I had my new teeth."

"Yes ma'am," I answered quietly, deciding it best to not rock the boat my first week in Nashville. "And don't worry, I'll pay my bills on time." I pushed back my chair and headed for the door.

I stepped back out onto the sidewalk of Eighth Avenue and paused amid the hustle and bustle of downtown Music City, USA, anxious to catch my breath and reflect on what had just taken place. I had been warned, but it hadn't sunk in. It had happened, but I still wasn't sure I believed it. Suddenly, standing there alone, I had a thought:

What would the lady have said had I written on the form that I was unemployed? I could have explained, "You see, ma'am, I've just gotten out of prison and I haven't been able to find a job just yet. I'm on parole after strangling my mother and slicing the neighbor's dog to bits with a meat cleaver. But I sure do need a telephone. I have to check in with my parole officer every day, you know."

A fan once asked Dolly Parton how long it takes to do her hair.
To which Dolly, famous for her wigs, replied, "I don't know. I'm never there."

"Why, of course, Mr. Anderson, you just sign here. We'll have your phone installed first thing tomorrow morning. Good thing you don't write music or entertain people, though. We'd have to charge you a $100 deposit.

"Have a nice day!"

Minnie Pearl got on an elevator one day with a man who thought he recognized her but wasn't sure. So he asked her guardedly, "Has anybody ever told you that you look like Minnie Pearl?"

Truthfully, Minnie answered, "Yes, they have."

To which the man replied, "Boy, don't that make you mad?"

CHAPTER TWO

Ah, my early days in Nashville and life in the country music business . . . . The late fifties, the sixties, on into the seventies. That twenty-odd year period of time between the invasion of rock 'n' roll and the invention of the Urban Cowboy. The days before there were very many interstate highways and no converted Silver Eagle busses at all. There were no twenty-four-track recordings, compact discs, music videos, tight playlists, twenty-page contract riders, development deals, road managers, or country music publicists. Telephones were not for sale at every checkout counter in America, and for those in our business, there was hardly any respect. Barbara Mandrell wouldn't sing about it for years to come, but we were country at a time when being country and singing country music for a living was not particularly cool.

And it wasn't just the people in Nashville who picked on us either. One cold and wintry afternoon a few years later, I discovered there were certain ones among "them" who also didn't want "us" staying in their hotels or motels either. And this happened a thousand miles away from Tennessee.

It wasn't that I was overly anxious to stay in this particular run-down motel where I was attempting to register in the first place, but it was the only game in town. It was late in the day, our show would start in a couple of hours, and my road-weary band members and I needed a place to shave, shower, and get a fresh start on the evening.

"I'm tellin' you for the last time," the little fat man bellowed from behind the check-in desk, "we don't allow no country music people to stay in this here motel. We run a nice, respectable place!"

"But *why* can't we stay here?" I begged for at least the third time. The first two times he had pretended not to hear me. "There's only five of us and we're not going to even mess up the beds. All we need is some soap, a few towels, and an hour and a half at the most, then we'll be gone. I'll pay you in cash."

"Look, Zeke, or Sonny Bubba, or whatever your name is. We don't allow no hillbilly singers here, understand? Last bunch we had in here liked to have tore this place to bits. We can't afford that no more."

"Who was it?" I asked, determined to convince him that Bill Anderson and The Po' Boys would be different.

"That ain't important. But they was country singers. You guys are all alike anyhow."

"But who?" I persisted.

"Never mind."

"Come on, who was it?"

"OK, if you have to know I'll tell you. It was Fats Domino."

"Fats Domino?" I screamed. "Fats Domino? He's not country. For goodness sakes, he's . . . ."

I never got a chance to finish. He turned on his heels, hustled his huffing, puffing body through a narrow passageway at the far end of the counter, slammed the door behind him, and disappeared into the twilight. I ambled slowly back out to the car, shaking my head in disbelief and trying to figure out (a) what the band and I were going to do about a place to clean up and (b) what in the devil made that fellow think I was Fats Domino's soul brother?

I never found out. But I did come to learn that these same scenarios and dozens of others in the same key had been played out wherever country music had dared to travel since back in the days of Jimmie Rodgers, and they would be played out again and again in my life, from one end of the country to the other, for the next many-plus years.

Bill's first Nashville publicity photo

"I don't know *why* they let you musicians stay here," an irritable hotel maid said to me and a group of my cohorts one snowy afternoon in Canada as we lounged around inside the room she was attempting to clean. "You guys don't do nothin' 'cept talk about chasin' women and wipe your boots on the bedspread!" She was serious, but I couldn't keep from laughing.

And yet, laugh as I might, I

wasn't sure for a long time that I understood all that was going on. What was the source of this bias against country music and our people anyhow? What had we ever done to hurt anybody? All I wanted to do was pick and sing. I wasn't out to rip off anybody's telephone company or get shoe polish on their darned ole bedspreads.

I had never been part of a minority group before. Born white, Anglo-Saxon, and Protestant, I wasn't used to being the object of prejudice. I had grown up in South Carolina and Georgia loving country music, idolizing the stars. I thought everybody else did, too. When I was a kid, the country singers and country musicians were among my very first heroes. Texas Jim Robertson was as big in my eyes as Babe Ruth; Al Dexter was on a par with General Douglas McArthur.

And now here I was living in Nashville, trying my best to

In his early show-biz days in Missouri, Porter Wagoner once waited backstage for his concert to begin, only to be told by the promoter, "The crowd's not coming in too well, so we're gonna hold the start of the show for awhile. I wonder if you'd mind going out on stage and telling the people that the show will be a little late in starting?"

Porter said he would, but first he walked to the stage and peeked through the curtain to see for himself just how many people were in the audience. He saw and returned to his dressing room without having said a word.

About a half hour later, the promoter came around again. "We still don't have enough people to start the show," he said. "Please go out and tell the audience we're going to wait just a bit longer."

"I've looked," Porter answered. "I know how many people's in here. And I'm not going out there. But if you'll go out there and get him and bring him back here, then I'll tell him!"

get established in the music business as a songwriter and a recording artist myself, longing to take my musical message to the world, and all I was running into was a whole lot of people who weren't nearly as enamored with my chosen profession as I was.

"Excuse me a minute, sir," the druggist had said to me when I first walked into a little drugstore in Minneapolis. "I'll be with you in a moment. But let me go turn my radio down. Someone turned it onto that doggone country music station again. I don't know who keeps doing that, but I don't want to offend any of my customers. I'll be right back."

"Hey, country music doesn't offend me at all," I offered. "Leave it on. I kinda like it."

"Really?" the druggist exclaimed, stopping cold in his tracks and turning

For years, people in our business have tried, without much success, to define country music. Founding members of the Country Music Association recall early days when the association spent most of its time attempting to describe the music it was trying to promote. To this day, there is still not a clear-cut definition as to exactly what country music is.

Songwriter John D. Loudermilk has his own idea: "If the money comes through a Nashville bank," he says, "then it's country."

around. He obviously had no idea who I was, or that I was the headline attraction that week at the country music theater across the street.

"Really," I affirmed.

"You know what?" he said, softening his voice, walking back toward me, and leaning out over the counter. "I like it, too. But most of the people who trade here don't care for it, so I try to not have it playing very loud when they come in."

"What you need is a bunch of new customers," I laughed, as the mellow tones of Hank Thompson's voice reverberated throughout the store.

"You're probably right," he concurred, and he laughed, too.

◆

In those days, country music not only received very little respect from members of the general public, but it was often held in even lower regard by people within other areas of the music business. Jazz drummer Buddy Rich, for example, delighted in putting down country music wherever he appeared. He was of the opinion that country musicians were inferior to musicians in other forms of music because most of us were not "musically schooled." His tirades on the "Tonight Show" against our people and our art form are legendary.

Supposedly, when Buddy Rich was in the hospital not long before his death, a nurse noticed he was especially uncomfortable and irritable one morning. She asked him, "Is something bothering you, Mr. Rich?"

To which Buddy is said to have replied, "Yes, country music."

I saw a similar type prejudice the day I first guested on the "Mike Douglas Show" on television. Mike had never had a country music act on his show at the time, but my recording of "Still" had crossed the boundaries from country music into pop, and his staff booked me to appear.

At the time, I was carrying only two musicians with me — Jimmy Lance on lead guitar and Weldon Myrick on steel. When the three of us arrived for rehearsal at the studio (Mike's show at the time was taped in Cleveland) and the musicians in the regular studio band spotted Weldon's steel guitar and my cow-

Mike Douglas and Bill

boy boots, one of them said sarcastically and in a voice loud enough for all to hear, "Well, this will set our show back ten years!"

Back home, I still couldn't figure out why country music had such limited acceptance in, of all places, Music City itself. Roy Acuff understood it, though. He once wrote: "Nashville, with all of its colleges and universities and high society, is a blue-blooded town. For a long time the elite people in this city would have liked to see the Opry destroyed and done away with. They thought it was belittling them."

Maybe that's why so many Nashvillians have, over the years, been slow to acknowledge their city's most famous product. "I've lived here all my life," my first next door neighbor boasted to me not long after I'd moved in, "and I've never set foot inside the Grand Ole Opry." His tone conveyed a sense of pride.

"I wish they'd stop calling Nashville 'Music City, USA'," a local shopkeeper said. "Everybody thinks we all walk around in Stetson hats and cowboy boots. It's bad for business."

A notable Nashville-born attorney says he attributes such remarks to jealousy.

And then there was the country singer who met a former neighbor on the streets of downtown Nashville. The neighbor was not current with the singer's career and asked to be brought up-to-date.

"Well, I've got a record in the top ten this week," the singer proudly told him.

"Wow!" said the neighbor. "I hadn't heard about that."

"And I've been nominated for a CMA Award!" the singer boasted.

"That's great!" exclaimed his friend. "I hadn't heard about that."

"Plus," the signer continued, "they're going to film a movie here next month, and I'm up for a major role!"

"That's wonderful," his friend conceded. "I hadn't heard about that. It sounds like everything in your life is perfect."

"Well, I played a show in Alabama last week and drew only a hundred people," the singer confessed.

"Yeah," said his neighbor, "I heard about that."

"That's it, plain and simple," he once told me. "Nashvillians are jealous."

"Of what?" I asked him.

"Of country music people and their success. I've lived here all my life, and I've seen families struggle and save in order to send their children to fine schools—like Vanderbilt University— to get an education. In addition, they've sometimes ended up having to sacrifice even more for long years of law school or medical school. And then these same, hard-working families look around one day and see some rhinestone cowboy who barely got out of the fifth grade moving in down the street. He's got a bigger house, he's driving a fancier car, and he's running around town with all the best looking women. And they're jealous of it. They know they can't fight it, so they turn their backs on it and pretend the whole country music scene doesn't exist."

To this day it rankles certain Nashvillians, when travelling to other cities around the world, to be asked where they are from.

"Oh, you're from Nashville!" people from Los Angeles to London will reply excitedly. "That's the home of the Grand Ole Opry, isn't it?" They utter nary a word about Vanderbilt University, the Parthenon, the Hermitage (home of President Andrew Jackson) or the dozens of other attractions of which Nashville is justifiably proud. But they will unashamedly ask, "You ever met Dolly Parton?"

Admittedly, there are—and always have been—*some* country music fans in Nashville, but not many of them have been among the city's business, civic, and social leaders. With that in mind, I have been puzzled for years as to how and why, one night back in the sixties, a group of notable Nashvillians came to hire me to perform at a posh banquet for the men and women who made up the leadership of the printing industry in Nashville. But they did. And, as you might suspect, before the night was over the highbrows and the hillbillies found themselves locked in an intriguing face-off.

It was a black-tie affair held at a swanky west Nashville country club, and I don't remember ever feeling quite so out of place, driving up the winding, landscaped driveway in my dilapidated green and white tour bus with "The Bill Anderson Show" painted in bright red letters down the side. I gingerly made my way inside the shiny marble foyer dressed in my aqua-colored rhinestone suit and my well-worn black and white, pointed-toe cowboy boots, more than a little fearful and with not the slightest idea of what to expect.

By show time, however, I had psyched myself into believing this was just another audience waiting to be entertained, and I hit the stage determined to pick 'n' grin and sing and charm the super-sophisticates right out of their rented tuxedos. But their frozen faces and meek, polite applause told me right away that these folks weren't going to be easily overwhelmed by the tall kid from Georgia and the plaintive country songs he had come to sing. I interpreted their indifference as their way of telling me they thought they were better than I was. And I didn't like that at all.

After the third or fourth song, I signalled for the band to stop and I faced the audience. "You know, you folks are some of the luckiest people in America," I said, quivering inside but smiling all the way. "Do you realize that you live in a city where millions of people all over the world would love to live? Nashville, Tennessee—the country music capital of the world! How many of you folks ever been to the Grand Ole Opry?" Just as I anticipated, not one hand in the crowd of several hundred went up. I turned to the band.

"Guys, did you know that the printing industry is Nashville's largest industry? It's bigger than the music business, the insurance business, banking, anything. The ladies and gentlemen in this room represent the cream of the crop in printing. How many of you guys ever been to a printing plant?" Nobody in the group raised their hand. My point was made. I turned back to the hushed crowd.

"Well, folks, it looks like we're starting off even," I said. "You don't know anything about us and we don't know anything about you. But that's no reason for us not to get along with one another. What say y'all just relax, listen to our music, and give us a chance to entertain you? You'll learn about us and we'll learn about you. At the end of evening, we're liable to find out we like each other."

We quickly kicked the music back into high gear and the ice was broken. We sang and we told jokes, and they began to tap their toes and smile and sing along with us, and it turned into a marvelous party. When the show was over, dozens of people from the audience stopped by the bandstand to tell us how much they enjoyed our performance. And again it was just as I had suspected.

"I've been to the Grand Ole Opry," many of them told me. "I just didn't want to be the only one to raise my hand. I was afraid the others might laugh at me."

"Well, I used to work for a newspaper myself," I confessed, "and I've been in dozens of printing plants. But I wasn't going to put myself on your level if you folks weren't willing to put yourselves on mine." I laughed and they laughed and we shook hands and parted as friends.

On my way home, I tried to sort it all out in my mind. Early in the evening, these people had acted cold, almost antagonistic, toward me. I, in turn, had grown defensive and alienated toward them. And then there we were, at the end of the night, patting each other on the back and visiting like long lost buddies. I decided that the catalyst for our ultimately coming together had most assuredly been the music.

And I smiled as I thought of Governor Jimmie Davis of Louisiana and the words he had spoken to a country music convention not long before. He was right.

"When people are singin'," the governor had said, "they ain't fightin'."

Show business, by its very nature, tends to be a business of hype and exaggeration. If a movie grosses a million dollars at the box office, immediately people connected with the film are out spreading the word that it's grossed over two-million. A phonograph record sells fifty thousand copies on Friday, and by Monday word on the street has it that the record is about to go gold—one million copies.

It's not a new phenomenon. That early country lyricist, William (Billy Bob) Shakespeare, probably sat with his buddies inside the Stratford-on-Avon Pub and told them over a hot chicken-fried steak and cold Budweiser that "Hamlet" was opening in Moscow when, in fact, Richard Burton had not yet even signed on for Broadway. With that in mind, picture this story that has been making the rounds in our business for years:

One of the top country music stars in all the world was booked into a terrible venue in a highly depressed town, and onto a show that had no promotion and advertising whatsoever. As a result, only four people showed up for his concert.

When the curtain went up, he could see there were only four seats filled in the entire theater, but being the pro that he was, he went ahead and performed his entire show just as if the theater were packed.

When he returned home the next day his wife asked him how the concert had gone. "Terrible," he answered. "Hardly anybody came to the show."

"Really?" she said. "How many were there?"

The star shook his head, looked down at the floor, and said sadly, "Only nine!"

Musicians can be unmerciful toward other musicians when talking about the instruments they play. The punch lines are all the same, only the instrument changes depending on who is telling the story. For some reason, however, accordion players and banjo players seem to take the brunt of most jokes:

For example: "Do you know the difference between an accordion and a trampoline?"

"No, what?"

"You take off your shoes when you jump on a trampoline!"

Or:

"Do you know what you call ten banjos lying on the bottom of the Mississippi River?"

"What?"

"A good start."

Or:

"Do you know the epitome of optimism? That's an accordion player with a beeper!"

Something you'll never hear at a recording session: "That's the banjo player's Porsche parked out back!"

Or Porter Wagoner's definition of a gentleman: "A man who can play an accordion but doesn't."

CHAPTER THREE

The city's prejudices and her idiosyncracies notwithstanding, I've always figured I arrived in Nashville at just the right time. A new era was dawning in country music, but the old era still had a foot in the door. On any given day there was a marvelous mixture of yesterday and tomorrow stirring the pot.

The first generation of country music superstars was still at the top of its game: Roy Acuff, Eddy Arnold, Ernest Tubb, Red Foley, Lefty Frizzell, Little Jimmy Dickens, Webb Pierce, Carl Smith, Hank Snow, Kitty Wells, Ray Price, Faron Young, Jim Reeves, Johnny Cash, Marty Robbins, Ferlin Husky, and all the rest. By the time I came onto the scene their music was legend, their names household words.

But new names were beginning to crop up: Roger Miller, Mel Tillis, Loretta Lynn, Don Gibson, Harlan Howard, Tom T. Hall, Hank Cochran, Willie Nelson, John D. Loudermilk, Marijohn Wilkin, and a guy named Bill Anderson—people who wrote their own songs and then went out on stage and sang them. In his autobiography, TV host Ralph Emery wrote that

Young Bill and Marty Robbins

"**D**o you know Merle Haggard?" a man once asked me at a personal appearance. "Sure," I replied.

"Then give this to him the next time you see him," he said, reaching into his pocket and handing me his business card. "Tell him I can cure his sinus problem."

"I didn't know Merle had a sinus problem," I offered, seeking additional insight.

"He sure does," the man insisted," and if you'll have him call me at the number on that card I'll cure him."

I promised that I would, and placed the card in my jacket pocket without reading it. I assumed the gentleman was a pharmacist or perhaps a doctor of some kind.

Later that night when the crowd had dispersed and I was alone, I removed the card from my coat and read it for the first time. I decided not to give the card to Merle. He might have a sinus problem, but I didn't think it was bad enough for this man to try and help him. The card was from Mabel's Septic Tank Service.

". . . country music got its greatest infusion of talent in the 1960s." The entire industry was on the verge of a transfusion of new blood, new creative sources, and new energy.

And yet, as much as I loved Nashville and as much as I wanted to live in and be a part of Music City, I came to town with my suitcase packed. For a long time, I didn't have a whole lot of desire to unpack it.

Sure, I wanted to write songs, I wanted to make records, I wanted to perform on the Grand Ole Opry, but like ninety percent of the other hopefuls drifting into town, more than anything else I wanted to throw my guitar across my back and seek my fame and fortune as a travelling troubadour. I wanted to hit the road.

Let's face it—the road has always been what country music is all about. Somebody once said that vaudeville never died, it just moved to Nashville. The surest sign of "making it" in country music has always been to have a calendar with a couple of hundred personal appearance dates penciled in for the year.

In the beginning, I'm not sure why being "on the road" sounded so exciting, so inviting to me, but it did. I hadn't travelled very much in my young life, but it wasn't the countryside I particularly wanted to see. It was the mystique I had built up in my mind about riding the wind, living like a gypsy, warming my soul by the heat of the footlights, abandoning my uncertainties inside the tumultuous roar of the crowd. Not to mention being part and parcel of all that took place on the back side of that mysterious velvet curtain.

Like the time the late Stringbean (Dave Akeman) came back to the dressing room following one of his musical and comedy performances that hadn't registered particularly well with the audience. We had heard his show through the walls, and we knew the applause and laughter for his songs and jokes had been somewhere between slim and none. String was never the type to get upset about much of anything, but we were a bit unsure as to just what kind of mood he would be in when he came off stage.

We shouldn't have worried. He was unflappable. He simply walked into the dressing room, laid his banjo in its case, lit his ever-present pipe, and walked over to where I sat in a folding chair. He stood there a minute, his lanky six-foot frame carrying not more than 150-pounds, towering over me. His tailor-made striped shirt hung down around his kneecaps, held in place by the belt on his tiny trousers that barely rose two feet above his shoe tops. His trademark, squared-off squashed-flat hat sat cocked to the side of his head. He extended his right arm, palm up, slowly down into my face. Ever so gently he began to rotate the palm until it faced the floor. And with a deadpan expression that would have done Buster Keaton proud, he said simply, "Chief, they took me serious!"

◆

Roger Miller was sitting in the dressing room one night following a similar experience with his comedy material. It had not gone over well at all. He was hanging his head a bit when a man who had been in the audience peeked into the dressing room and blurted out, "Roger, you were great! It was all I could do to keep from laughing!"

◆

And the late Archie Campbell, of "Hee-Haw" fame, used to tell of working a show years ago at a small-town school house in upper east Tennessee. Several of the top stars from the Grand Ole Opry were there, and the little auditorium was packed to the rafters. But each act went on stage and came off shaking their head. Nobody in the audience was applauding. Nobody in the audience was laughing at the jokes. It was like the artists were performing inside a funeral parlor.

When the show ended, all the acts gathered around and began trying to figure out what they had done wrong. Was the sound system distorted? Could the people not hear? Did they not like country music? What was the problem?

As they searched among themselves for answers, a local law enforcement officer sauntered up, a big dude standing about six-foot five and weighing well over two-hundred pounds. He puffed out his chest, hooked his thumbs inside the belt loops on his uniform trousers and asked, "Well, how'd you folks like our little town?"

Nobody was in a hurry to reply. Finally, someone spoke up and said, "Well, it sure was a quiet audience."

"You darn right it was," the big policeman answered. "I been telling people 'round here, 'Last show we had here, you folks got plum rowdy. Now, these stars are comin' a long way, and we're gonna show 'em some respect. First one of you makes a sound, I'm gonna throw you in jail!' Nice polite crowd, wasn't it boys?"

◆

I've been asked a million times why I've chosen to put up with all the hassles and inconveniences of working the road all these years when I could have easily stayed in Nashville, written songs for a living, and enjoyed a peaceful and comfortable existence. My reply is now and has always been: Nobody applauds when you write a song.

Applause surely must be the most powerful aphrodisiac known to mankind. The quest for it is a disease of the blood. Or, at best, a genetic disorder. What else would cause an apparently rational person of sound body and mind to pack his belongings and heedlessly ride away from his spouse and family in order to pursue such a nomadic and pointless existence? I mean, it's not like entertainers cure cancer or anything.

Or do we?

I once rode all night and half a day through a blinding snowstorm only to arrive in the little North Dakota town where we were booked to perform to find our concert had been cancelled due to the weather. A handful of people hadn't heard the news, however, and had managed somehow to brave the elements and make their way to the auditorium.

Normally, under such circumstances, no one would expect the entertainers to perform. All performance contracts contain an "Act Of God" clause which states that if something out of human control occurs, the contract becomes null and void. Obviously, human beings cannot control the weather.

The promoter was under no obligation to pay us for the date. Likewise, we had no obligation to go on stage. We were cold, we were tired and hungry. The endless miles on a narrow, snowswept highway had taken their toll. But there was something in the eyes of those few fans who had shown up that told us how badly they wanted to hear the music they knew we could play if only we would.

There was a small kitchen off to the side of the auditorium, and the promoter offered to cook us some food. We warmed our hands by the steam heat rising off a small group of antiquated radiator coils in the corner of the hallway and talked the situation over. There was certainly no place else for us to go. The entire town was held prisoner by the storm. Why not drink some coffee, fill our bellies, and pick a little country music?

Which is exactly what we did. I told the audience they'd better treat us real good, though, because we had 'em outnumbered. We gave to them of our time and our talents and, in return, they were more than generous to us with their applause.

Country singer on a show promoter he didn't trust:

"I'd rather have him after me with a shotgun than with a pencil."

When our show was over, we stood around for awhile and signed a few autographs and visited with the people. An elderly lady, wearing a heavy coat that had obviously kept her warm for many long winters, her head wrapped in a faded blue scarf, approached the stage where I was standing.

"You don't know how much this evening has meant to me," she said, reaching up for my hand and looking deeply into my eyes.

"Well, we've enjoyed it, too," I replied, smiling and giving her hand a slight squeeze.

"My husband just passed away," she said sadly, lowering her head. "I haven't been out of the house since he died except to go to the grocery and to church. I didn't really want to come here today, but my daughter insisted on bringing me. My husband and I had lots of your records, and we used to enjoy so much watching you on TV."

I smiled and thanked her.

"I'm so glad to get to meet you," she continued. "Thank you for playing and singing for such a small crowd. Today is the first time I have smiled since my husband died. Your music has helped me to forget my problems for awhile."

OK, so entertainers don't cure cancer. But maybe, every once in a while, we cure some other things that are almost as important.

Our business is full of weather-related stories. Once, years ago, my plane couldn't land in San Francisco due to a heavy fog blanketing the Bay Area. I was scheduled to perform at eight o'clock that night at a small club about an hour from the airport. I was already an hour late when the plane finally landed. By the time I reached the club, it was after ten and the crowd was beginning to disperse. The owner was refunding their money.

A big dude in a white ten-gallon hat was just leaving the club when I arrived. He spotted me and ran back inside to tell the owner I was there. The owner's reaction was, "Well, it's too late. The show's off."

But this guy and most of the people, many of whom were still milling around

For several decades following his death, country disc jockeys constantly referred to Hank Williams as "the late and great Hank Williams." The phrase became ingrained in listerners' minds.

Jimmy Gateley once had a man say to him, "You know, I believe I like that Mr. Late Hank Williams better than I did that first Mr. Hank Williams."

inside or out on the sidewalk, wanted to hear me sing. That's what they had come for. They begged the owner to change his mind. "He can sing if he wants to," the boss said, "but I'm not gonna pay him."

"Well, I will," retorted the big cowboy, whereupon he took off his large hat and tossed a twenty dollar bill inside. "C'mon folks," he yelled to the crowd, "this guy has had a rough night. It wasn't his fault the plane couldn't land in the fog. He's here now and he wants to sing. Whatta you say we pay him to sing?" And he began to pass the hat around the suddenly crowded room.

I couldn't believe it. By the time the house band got back on stage, tuned up, and I handed them a list of my songs, the hat was overflowing with money. When I counted it, there was more than twice as much money as my contract with the owner had called for.

I sang until after two o'clock in the morning.

◆

Many years later, at a county fair in New Jersey, about halfway through our performance it began to pour down rain. The audience was seated across a race track from the stage inside a covered grandstand. They were protected and dry. We were set up on a concrete slab that served as a stage and were totally exposed.

Just as soon as the musicians in my band began to feel the first drops of rain, they immediately unplugged their electrical instruments and ran for cover inside our bus. Our sound engineer unplugged the amplifiers and speakers and sought cover himself. We huddled inside the front lounge of the bus, listening to the raindrops pounding the roof. It was a vicious storm.

We hadn't been back on the bus five minutes when the door flung open and the promoter of the show barged inside. "What do you mean stopping the show?" he roared. "The audience is furious. They're over there stomping and whistling. They came to see a show. You're not going to melt. Get back out there!"

I moved to try and calm him down. "Sir, there's a lot of water out on that stage right now," I said, pointing to a deep puddle where the guitar player had been standing. "Our instruments and sound system pull a tremendous amount of electricity onto that stage. It would be very, very dangerous for us to be out there right now."

He was totally insensitive to our plight. "Look," he screamed, "in the entire history of the music business, there has only been *one* guitar player ever killed playing in the rain!"

To which my guitar player immediately replied, "Yes sir, and we intend to keep it that way."

◆

For an entertainer, the constant touring—being away from home night after night, waking up in a different town each morning, always eating in restaurants, sleeping on a bus or in a strange bed every night—can often be discombobulating and wearing on the mind. After awhile, the days, the towns, the concerts all start running together.

The story goes that a major star, in the midst of a long tour, once telephoned his wife to check on things back in Nashville. "And how's our son?" the star asked.

There was a long pause on the other end of the line. "Uh . . . our son's on the tour with you," his wife replied.

"Oh, yes, that's right," the star said. "He's fine. Just fine."

◆

When an artist is on the road, it's also very easy to lose track of special occasions, like birthdays, anniversaries, and dates that otherwise might be significant. Away from home, the days and nights often come and go in one big blur.

I would have never told this story during his or his parents' lifetimes, but I was once on tour with Red Foley when he forgot a date he had wanted badly to remember.

It was the Monday following Mother's Day, and we were in his hotel room in Prince George, British Columbia, Canada. Somewhere in the course of our conversation, I happened to casually mention that I had called my mother the day before to wish her a Happy Mother's Day.

"Was yesterday Mother's Day?" Red asked me.

I assured him that it was.

"Oh, no," he said, hanging his head and dropping his gaze to the floor. "I forgot to call Mama."

I tried to console him. "Well, I'm sure she knows you were thinking of her," I said. "Besides, we're not exactly in Kentucky."

He didn't say a word, he just kept staring at the floor. In a moment, he turned and stretched his body across the bed and pulled the telephone off the night stand on the other side. With a deep sigh and a forlorn look on his face he picked up the receiver.

"I'd like to place a call to Berea, Kentucky, in the United States," he told the operator. And he gave her the number.

For a long time he sat in silence on the side of the bed, cradling the phone against his ear. I got up and started for the door in an effort to give him some privacy, but he motioned for me to sit back down. Neither of us spoke.

In a few minutes he gave the operator a series of numbers which I assumed to be his credit card. Suddenly his face lifted and his eyes brightened.

"Mama?" I heard him say into the phone. "Mama, is that you? This is Clydie."

His full name was Clyde Julian Foley, and to his mother and father he had never been "Red." He had always been "Clydie."

"I'm so glad I was able to get through to you, Mama" he continued. "I couldn't let the day get by without calling to wish you a Happy Mother's Day."

Silence. It seemed to last a long time.

"Yesterday? What do you mean Mother's Day was yesterday? Mama, I'm calling you from British Columbia and up here Mother's Day is *today*." He sounded heartbroken. I looked into the corner of his eye and saw the beginnings of a tear.

More silence, finally broken by a choked voice.

"Well, Mama, I'm really sorry if Mother's Day was yesterday in Kentucky. But up here in British Columbia it's today. You know I'd never forget you, Mama. I'd never forget to call on Mother's Day. You know that, don't you?" Then a quick change of subject: "How's Papa?"

The conversation continued for several more minutes and I could sense the mood beginning to slowly grow warmer and more light-hearted, at least on our end. In a few minutes I heard him say, "Well, I've got to go now, Mama. I love you and Papa. Happy Mother's Day."

Red Foley hung up the phone, looked at me, and began to sob like a baby. "I hate myself when I do things like that," he cried. "Honest to God. I hate myself."

◆

The road can sometimes play other tricks on your mind. Many is the story of an entertainer being booked in Springfield, Illinois, and travelling by mistake to Springfield, Missouri. Or Springfield, Ohio. The same holds true with Charleston, South Carolina and Charleston, West Virginia. Jim Ed Brown once took driving to the wrong town to new heights.

It was in the days when he was recording and touring with his sisters, Maxine and Bonnie, as The Browns. They were scheduled to begin a long western tour with Slim Whitman, Wanda Jackson, and myself in Pocatello, Idaho. The second night of the tour we were to be 117 miles up the road in Twin Falls.

The Browns had driven straight through to Idaho from Nashville, and by the time they reached Pocatello around noon on the day of the first show, they were tired. So tired, in fact, that Jim Ed, who was driving the car, became confused and thought the tour opened in Twin Falls. He drove right on through Pocatello and arrived in mid-afternoon at a motel in Twin Falls.

"You're here kind of early, aren't you?" the desk clerk asked as Jim Ed filled out the registration card.

"No, not really," Jim Ed replied, checking his watch. "We'll just barely have time to clean up and eat before the show starts."

"But your show's not until tomorrow night," the clerk informed him.

"Tomorrow night? Where are we?" Jim Ed quickly realized his mistake.

He raced out of the motel, jumped back in the car, and high-tailed it across those same 117 miles back to Pocatello. The Browns barely got to the auditorium by show time. It was three days into the tour before Jim Ed got around to admitting to the rest of us what had happened.

◇

In the days when country entertainers travelled to all their personal appearance dates in automobiles, practical jokes among the band members were a way of life. The physical closeness of five or six musicians cramped into one car, the endless miles, the boredom all played a part.

Hank Snow's band members once left Los Angeles around midnight at the end of a long west-coast tour headed for Nashville. Everybody in the group was worn out, but one member of the group volunteered to take the first shift driving, provided another of the other musicians would promise to relieve him promptly at six o'clock in the morning. One of the guys said he would, if he could get into the back seat right then and go to sleep. A deal was struck.

The would-be relief driver had been asleep for only a short while when another band member seated in the rear cautiously reached over and set the sleeping man's wristwatch forward six hours. The lights of L.A. were barely out of sight when the driver pulled into a rest stop and woke his buddy.

"Time to wake up," he prodded, gently poking the unsuspecting musician in the ribs. "Your turn to drive."

The relief driver yawned and stretched and tried to clear the cobwebs from his mind. "Gee, what time is it?" he asked. "I don't feel like I've been asleep more than an hour."

"It's six o'clock," the driver answered. "Check your watch." Sure enough, the young man's watch read six o'clock. He got out, walked around the car, and wearily climbed in under the wheel. Driver Number One slid quickly into the back seat and promptly fell asleep.

Driver Number Two says he never suspected a thing for the first hundred miles or so. "But when the sun hadn't come up by ten o'clock," he confessed, "I knew I'd been had!"

◇

Bill, on the road again

By the mid to late sixties, most of the major country artists had gone from travelling to their concert dates sitting upright in crowded automobiles and station wagons to reclining in comfort aboard large, customized tour busses. With the coming of the busses came a whole new approach to touring and the addition of a new, heretofore-unnecessary member of the travelling entourage—the tour bus driver.

There are as many bus driver stories as there are bus drivers, but one of my favorites took place the day my regular driver, James Price, became ill only hours before we were scheduled to pull out for a long tour through the midwest. We had to find a substitute driver and we had to find one in a hurry.

My road manager, my secretary, and I all hit the phones and began calling everyone we could think of in an effort to find someone who could leave town on extremely short notice and be gone a couple of weeks. None of us was turning up anything, and the hours were rapidly ticking away.

Finally, in desperation, the road manager picked up the evening newspaper and began scouring the want-ads. A quick phone call later he came charging into my office screaming, "I've done it! I found one! I found us a driver!" I thought he was going to pass out from sheer jubilation.

I didn't ask him any questions. He had found a driver. That was all I needed to know. I left the office and headed home to pack. I arrived back at the bus a couple of hours later, exhausted but happy our problem had been solved.

Our new driver was seated in the driver's seat when I climbed aboard the bus. I didn't pay him a whole lot of attention, just shook his hand, thanked him for adjusting his schedule with so little advance warning, and headed for my bunk and some much-needed sleep. It had been a trying day.

I didn't give the bus nor the driver another thought until well after daybreak the next morning when I stumbled into the forward lounge of the bus to pour myself a cup of coffee. It was only then, when I looked toward the window in the driver's bulkhead at the front of the bus, that I realized I couldn't see anyone seated at the wheel. I knew there had to be a driver up there somewhere, though, because we were roaring down the interstate and seemingly staying between the lines. I knew the bus was not equipped with automatic pilot.

I slowly made my way toward the front, peeked around the thin wall that separated the driver from his passengers and found myself staring upon what will be the strangest scene I hope ever to witness at seventy miles an hour. There, behind the wheel of my bus, *stood* the bus driver. He was not sitting down as most drivers would be, but was standing—his tiny arms struggling to reach across the steering wheel—as we charged down the road.

I immediately realized why. Had he been sitting in the driver's seat, his legs would have come up about six inches short of the pedals on the floor. In our haste to find a bus driver who could both leave town on a moment's notice and be gone for two weeks, we had hired a midget! An honest-to-goodness, bona fide, card-carrying midget!

I didn't know whether to laugh or to cry. The little fella wasn't four feet tall. He looked like a rag doll someone had propped up and draped across the wheel—like he should have been *in* a show somewhere, not driving us to one. All I could think was, "Good Lord, my life is in the hands of a dwarf!"

It wasn't all that funny at the time, but I can laugh about it now. The midget (who we immediately nicknamed "Shorty") turned out to be a delightful man. He confessed to having lied when the road manager had asked him on the phone if he had ever driven a bus, but he said he lied only because he was stone broke and desperate for a job. "I did drive a truck once," he said, but when I pressed him, he admitted it was a dump truck and all he had done was haul dirt across town.

We kept Shorty with us for the entire tour, but the only driving I let him do was from the motels to the shows. I taught him to sell souvenirs. I figured it was safer to have a midget hawking my albums than hauling my body!

Harlan Howard, perhaps country music's most consistently prolific songwriter, has been married six times. "I stay married until I run out of songs," he once said.

Harlan was recently invited to the home of another songwriting legend, Curly Putman. "It was magnificent," Harlan reported after the visit.

"His house is a mansion. It sits high on a hill overlooking hundreds of acres of rolling pasture land. Curly cooked me breakfast and we relaxed and enjoyed the spectacular scenery. Later in the day, he took me out to his yacht. It's beautifully furnished, and again we relaxed, and Curly cooked me a steak.

"It got me to thinking: Hell, I should have married Curly!"

Harlan Howard with Bill

CHAPTER FOUR

One of the things that grabbed my attention when I first arrived on the music scene—a would-be travelling minstrel man—was the excitement of all the big new coliseums and civic centers that were being built and beginning to open in major cities all across North America. These shiny new edifices extended an open invitation to enterprising concert promoters everywhere to experiment with a new format of presenting live entertainment to the public—the package show.

Actually, a package show was nothing new and was no more than the coming together on the same stage of a large number of artists who normally did not appear in concert together. Small package shows had been in existence for years, but with the coming of the super auditoriums, for the first time it became economically feasible to "package' and present the biggest of the superstars on the same bill.

For the fans, package shows were the bargain of all bargains. I ran across a newspaper ad not long ago for a tour I worked across western Canada in the winter of 1961. The stars, in the order they were advertised, were Marty Robbins, Stonewall Jackson, Bill Anderson, Warren Smith, Jimmy C. Newman, Roger Miller, Don Winters, and a comedian known simply as Goober. For some reason there was no female singer, usually a staple on every package show, but there were eight featured acts and the highest priced reserved seat ticket cost two dollars! General admission was a dollar seventy-five, and children under twelve could get in for a dollar. Imagine a show with comparable star-power today. Fans would have to sell the farm and leave the kids at a pawn shop just to be able to afford to come see it!

A package group: (L-R) Marty Robbins, Jean Shepard, Hawkshaw Hawkins and Bill.

Package shows, for all their star-studded drawing power, had one inherent problem: There were often so many acts on the bill that the shows themselves ran far too long.

The performers would be instructed to stay on stage for only x-number of minutes so that each act would have a fair amount of time to perform and still allow the show to be over at a reasonable hour, but it hardly ever worked out that way. A long-winded emcee would get carried away and forget the audience had come to hear the singers and not him. One of the featured acts would lose track of his or her alloted time and stay on stage too long. Or the sound system would go bonkers and bring everything to a grinding halt.

Sound systems in those days were a big barrel of laughs. And I say that with my tongue planted firmly against the inside of my cheek. We played and sang into whatever sound system was built into the auditorium, period. Virtually nobody carried their own sound equipment (Sonny James was one of the first to begin doing so), and the touring sound companies had not yet come into prominence. To make matters worse, very few of the big, new coliseums—fancy as they were—had been constructed with the thought in mind of reproducing clear, quality sound for musical performances. More often than not, we were forced to sing into the same microphones and have our voices come out through the same speakers the announcers used to describe the action at a basketball tournament or a hockey game. "Stopanivich goes to the penalty box for two minutes!" or "My mama sang a song." Into a dollar ninety-five microphone and out of a tin-horn speaker, they both sounded the same.

One of the first things an entertainer built into his repertoire, then, was a good supply of bad-sound-system jokes. "Gee, they spent ten million dollars on this beautiful building and hired Mickey Mouse to install the sound equipment!" was one that could always get a few laughs and a smattering of applause. That is, if the audience could hear the artist say it.

◆

Long shows were especially frustrating to the headline acts who would drive all the way to the date, sit in the dressing room while the opening acts ciphoned off most of the energy from the audience, and would then be left with only fifteen or twenty minutes on stage to perform before a lifeless crowd and an impending local curfew. I saw former Opry great Carl Smith come up with a unique solution to the problem one night.

We were working a package show in Milwaukee, along with a large contingent of other entertainers from Nashville, when a group of singers and dancers from the local area got carried away and stayed on stage far too long. Carl sat patiently backstage talking with me and glancing ever so often at his watch. A couple of minutes after midnight, he calmly broke off the conversation, put his guitar in its case, pulled on his overcoat, and headed for the exit without ever having gone on stage to perform.

"Where are you going?" the promoter, who had already paid Carl his fee, screamed. "You can't leave. You haven't gone on stage yet!"

"You hired me for a show *yesterday*!" Carl replied, pointing to a clock on the backstage wall which by that time registered nearly twelve fifteen A.M. "Check your copy of the contract." And with that, he calmly walked out of the building and into the night.

◆

Very few show promoters were as lax with performers running past their alloted time on stage as the promoter in Milwaukee. A crotchety old man named Ward Beam, who for years booked country acts into the major fairs in the northeast, took it to the opposite extreme.

Ward, who looked so much like my grandfather that I could never get mad at him, would always tell us precisely how long he wanted each of us to perform, and then he would pull out a stop-watch when we went on stage to make sure we adhered to his instructions. He once told me at a matinee performance to stay on stage "no more than seventeen minutes." I thought I had done exactly as he told me until I came down the steps backstage and he grabbed me by the arm. He began to shake me violently.

"You ran over!" he roared. "I told you to stay on for seventeen minutes and you were up there seventeen minutes and thirty-three seconds! Now, on the night show, you cut out that joke you told between your third and fourth songs and you'll be just right!" I did as I was told. I was afraid not to.

Another promoter once insisted that Ferlin Husky sing for "exactly one half-hour, no more and no less."

Ferlin, ever the clown, took an alarm clock on stage with him. He set the alarm, placed the clock on a podium off to the side of the stage, and began his show. In the middle of his closing song, "Wings Of A Dove," the alarm went off.

Ferlin immediately stopped singing, gathered up the clock, and left the stage. The promoter flew into a rage, insisting that Ferlin return to the screaming crowd and finish his signature song.

"My thirty minutes are up," Ferlin announced, and he refused to go back. His point was made.

◆

I would be less than honest if I didn't admit to having occasionally been guilty of running overtime on stage myself. I never meant to be disrespectful to the other acts, but show me an artist who's never done it. You get on stage and get excited, the adrenaline kicks in, and it's easy to lose track of time. I've had promoters get on my case backstage, but only once was I ever reprimanded in front of an audience. Once was enough.

The venue was an outdoor park called Buck Lake Ranch near Angola, Indiana, a place where fans would gather early on Sunday afternoons in the summertime for picnics and a day full of country music. The park was run by an elderly couple named Harry and Eleanor Smythe, and Harry was a stickler for punctuality. He wanted his shows to start on time and end on time, primarily because when the fans were sitting in the grandstand watching the shows they weren't out spending money riding his rides and eating at his concession stands.

I had wanted to work at Buck Lake Ranch ever since I had been in Nashville, but this was my first opportunity. I was excited. It was 1962, and the fates were smiling on me. I had the No. 1 record in the country, "Mama Sang A Song," and we had drawn a huge crowd. Plus, sharing the bill with me that day at Buck Lake Ranch were special friends, Jan Howard and the Carter Family.

"Mama Sang A Song" is a religious recitation that featured on the recording the beautiful background voices of the Anita Kerr Singers singing lines from such well-known hymns as "What A Friend We Have In Jesus," "Rock Of Ages," and "Precious Memories." It was a stunning arrangement, but it was proving to be a very difficult song for me to duplicate on stage because, naturally, I couldn't afford to carry a choir with me everywhere I went to perform.

On this particular Sunday, however, Jan and the Carter Family—Mama

Maybelle, Helen, and Anita—agreed to sing the background hymns with me. I was ecstatic. The Carters and Jan could blend harmonies as well as or better than anybody in country music. There was no doubt that "Mama Sang A Song" would be the highlight of my set. I decided to make it my closing song.

I did the first part of my show and glanced carefully at my watch as I called the Carters and Jan back on stage for the finale. I had about two minutes of my alloted time remaining. The song would take nearly four minutes, but I didn't worry. I figured nobody would complain if I ran two minutes too long. Especially with a performance as dynamic as I knew this was going to be.

Grandpa Jones once went to introduce singer Marion Worth on stage at the Opry and forgot her name. He could only remember her initials, plus the name of a long-time Opry sponsor. With no time on the live broadcast to turn and seek help, he simply leaned into the microphone and pleaded, "Let's have a big hand now for Miss Martha White!"

◆

More recently, on the nationally televised portion of the Opry, Grandpa was scheduled to introduce young Martina McBride. He was obviously not familiar with the work of this outstanding new country singer, and asked the audience to please give a nice welcome to "Miss Matilda McBride".

But I totally underestimated Harry Smythe and his obsession with his concession stands and time. About halfway through my recitation—just as I was getting to the part about daddy's back growing weak and mama's faith growing strong, just as the vocal group was easing into "Rock of Ages, Cleft For Me"—from out of nowhere I heard a booming voice. I knew immediately it wasn't God:

"All right, get off the stage! Right now! Get *off* the stage!"

I couldn't believe my ears. What was going on? Who would dare interrupt a song that way? Especially a religious song. I turned to my left where Jan and the Carters were backing away from the microphone in shock and there stood Harry Smythe, a microphone in one hand and a look of wild hysteria in both eyes. The music began to slowly die, one instrument at a time. The stage grew eerily quiet, the air thick and heavy with anticipation. Almost fear. The crowd clung to the edges of their seats, afraid to move. Were we in the presence of a mad-man?

I waited for him to speak again. "Boy," he roared, "you've stayed on this stage too long."

"But, I only had . . . ." I began, trying to explain that this would have been my last song and that I was almost through, and besides it was a religious recitation and I didn't feel he should have interrupted me.

"Get off here right now," he demanded without having heard one thing I said. And then he revealed the real reason for his anger: "My hamburgers are getting cold!" he thundered.

I would tell you what I told him he could do with his hamburgers, but I dedicated this book to my parents and they don't know I ever even *thought* of words like that.

◆

It is very important to an artist that he or she be properly introduced to the audience prior to coming on stage to perform. A good, up-beat introduction puts the crowd in a much better mood to respond than does a rambling, mundane preamble. And an artist who feels he or she has been properly introduced is much more likely to come out on stage in a positive frame of mind to perform.

For that reason, most entertainers prefer to have one of the members of their own travelling group bring them on stage rather than chance a poor introduction by an outsider.

Merle Haggard, however, once worked a date for a promoter who was quite star-struck. He made no secret of the fact that his biggest ambition in life was to walk out on stage prior to the concert and introduce Merle.

Merle, of course, had a stylized introduction to his show, and he didn't want anyone other than a member of his band bringing him on. This particular promoter was so insistent that he be allowed to introduce Merle, however, that Merle's manager finally relented.

"But we don't want you up there ad-libbing a fancy introduction, understand?" the manager said. "All you say is, 'Ladies and gentlemen—Here he is— the poet of the common man—Merle Haggard!' You got that? That's all you say!"

The promoter assured the manager that he understood perfectly.

Undoubtedly, he meant well. But when it came time to bring Merle on stage the promoter got excited and a bit flustered:

"Ladies and gentlemen," he roared into the microphone, "Here he is—The po' and common man, Merle Haggard!"

◆

For years the top promoter of country concerts in Miami and south Florida was a disc jockey known as Cracker Jim. Jim was a very nice man, had a big following of loyal listeners and fans in the Miami area, but an emcee for a live concert he was not. He was notorious for bringing artists on stage with all the enthusiasm of an embalmer.

I once stood in the wings and heard him drone, "And now here's Ernest

Tubb, and I hope you get a large charge."

My favorite Cracker Jim introduction, however, took place one night when Faron Young was the show's headline attraction and I was one of the "many others" also on the bill.

Faron knew he would be closing the show so he didn't feel it was important for him to be at the auditorium when the opening curtain went up. He knew there would be several acts on stage prior to him, so he went out for a leisurely dinner beforehand. No one in the audience would have known whether Faron Young was backstage waiting to go on stage or not, but Cracker Jim knew Faron wasn't in the building and he panicked.

As he would go out to introduce each of the opening acts, Cracker Jim would say, "Folks, the star of the show, Faron Young, isn't here yet. But don't worry, I know he'll be here. In the meantime, here's so-and-so." Cracker Jim couldn't have turned the audience any colder if he had thrown a bucket of ice water in their faces. The artists had to work twice as hard as they normally would just to get the slightest reaction from the crowd.

As Cracker Jim walked on stage to introduce me, however, Faron came walking in the back door. Jim actually got enthused:

"Folks, I've got great news! Faron Young is here! He just came in backstage and he'll be coming out here to entertain you real soon. Don't worry anymore, the great Faron Young is here!" Then he dropped his voice back into its customary monotone:

"In the meantime, here's Bill Anderson."

◆

Little Jimmy Dickens tells of once being brought on stage by an emcee who said, "Here's Little Jimmy Dickerson! . . . They tell me he's the king of the banjo!"

Jimmy Dickens never played a banjo in his life.

◆

Off-beat and hilarious introductions are not limited to country music. This one actually happened to a gospel music quartet.

It was a new group that had just recorded its very first album and was about to embark on its debut tour. The members had named themselves The Celestials, an appropriate word, they figured, relating to things spiritual and heavenly in nature.

But they suddenly and unwittingly had a change in plans. When the new album came in just prior to the group's leaving on the big tour, they were horrified to find the pressing plant had inadvertently inserted a "T" where there should have been a "C" in the group's name. Thousands of albums had been pressed calling the quartet the Telestials.

They were heartsick. They looked up "telestial" in the dictionary only to discover there wasn't any such word. But there was no time to change it. They had to make the best of a bad situation. The quartet that had started out to be the Celestials was now the Telestials, like it or not.

Came the night of their first performance, and as fate would have it, the man who was going to introduce them on stage for the very first time was an elderly preacher whose memory and eyesight were each failing him fast.

"What's the name of your group again?" he asked them backstage, just prior to opening the concert.

"The Telestials," they replied. "The Singing Telestials."

Not being familiar with the word, the aging minister asked if one of them would mind writing it down so he wouldn't forget it. One of the group obliged, and handed the preacher a slip of paper with "The Singing Telestials" written on it.

The old man took the paper, ambled onto the stage and up to the open microphone.

"Ladies and gentlemen," he began, "we've got a great treat for you tonight. I'm here to present a brand-new group making their very first personal appearance." He fumbled with the piece of paper in his hand and decided he'd best glance at it one more time, just to be sure. He strained to read the name, the bright glare of the spotlight blurring his vision. He struggled to make out the writing through his thick glasses.

He almost got it right, but not quite. "Please make welcome," he roared to the crowd, "a dynamic new group, The Singing Testicles!"

◆

As funny as that story is, I'm not sure any introduction will ever top the one I received the night an emcee completely forgot my name. In desperation she finally said, "Come on out here, boy, and tell 'em who you are!"

CHAPTER FIVE

The supporting acts on the package shows, those artists who were billed beneath the headline attraction, were always expected to know their place and usually they did. They were stars, but not *the* star.

One night Charley Pride, the hottest act in the business in the late sixties and early seventies, had been booked to headline a concert that featured, among others, the late Webb Pierce. Back in the fifties, Webb had had an unbelievable string of No. 1 records and had ruled the charts like no other artist. But this was twenty years later and Webb's popularity had waned. His current appeal couldn't have begun to match that of Charley Pride.

The massive auditorium was jammed when Webb and his entourage swept in backstage just before show time. I was standing with Charley talking to a group of fans when Webb spotted us and walked over. He stuck out his hand and said, "Hi, Charley. It sure is nice to have you on my show!"

There was a moment of awkward silence. I held my breath. It will be to Charley's eternal credit that he simply smiled and said, "Thanks, Webb. It's good to be with you."

There was no such thing as backstage security as we know it today back in the old package show days. Just about anybody who could find the backstage entrance and was clever enough to make up a good excuse could wander in.

"Roy Acuff is my uncle," was a good one. "Cousin Minnie Pearl really is my cousin!" was another. Or, as one would-be gate crasher told me one night, "I've got two uncles who play down there at the Grand Ole Opry."

"Is that right?" I said. "Who are they?"

> **B**ill Monroe has never been known as a man of many words. He has preferred, over the years, to let his world-renowned bluegrass music do most of the talking for him.
>
> The story goes that the late Clyde Moody, then a new member of Bill's famed Bluegrass Boys band, had trouble dealing with the fact that Bill would often travel for days on end without speaking to him. A car loaded with musicians can grow awfully small if the air is thick with tension. Clyde felt he had to speak to Bill about the silence.
>
> "Mr. Bill," he said one morning as the group was loading the car to leave on a long tour, "maybe I don't belong in this group. I've been with you several weeks now and you haven't even spoken to me."
>
> To which Bill replied, "Good morning, Clyde. Git in." And he never said another word.

"Earl Flatt and Earl Scruggs," he answered.

I laughed and waved him on in.

◆

Fans would often come backstage before the shows started and bring big baskets filled with food and drink for the stars. This became such a ritual at certain auditoriums that we'd get worried if we showed up in a particular place and the providers weren't there.

Symphony Hall in Newark, New Jersey, became a favorite stop on the circuit thanks to the "Chicken Ladies," a group of three or four women who would always bring home-cooked chicken dinners with all the trimmings backstage to the performers. The ladies became so well-known in that area that a major national magazine once dispatched a reporter to trail them to one of our concerts. The result was a big spread in the magazine, complete with photographs.

At the Keil Auditorium in St. Louis, where we worked many a Sunday matinee, we always knew there would be hot coffee, homemade sandwiches, and cookies waiting for us in a dressing room upstairs. At the outdoor parks and fairs, groups of fans were always getting together fan club picnics, each member trying to out-cook the other. We'd stuff our faces and get back home weighing ten pounds more than when we left. One day, at one of the outdoor country music parks, I counted sixteen cakes and pies baked by fans and brought to our bus. We couldn't possibly eat them all, so when the show was over we picked out a few to take home and then drove over to a nearby children's hospital and gave the others to the kids.

Most artists have it in their contracts today that backstage food has to be provided by the promoters. None of us ever thought to ask for something like that then. Maybe we were naive to dig in and eat whatever people brought us, but so far as I know, no one ever tried to poison us.

Well, maybe they did try. They just never succeeded.

◆

The great country-blues singer Narvel Felts and I were reminiscing not long ago about our days on tour together, and the subject of food came up.

He grinned his big ole Missouri grin and asked me, "Do you remember the night in Syracuse when the people invited us out to the VFW Club for a steak dinner after the show?"

I thought a minute but couldn't recall.

"Don't you remember? It was me and you and Jack Greene and Kenny Price. Jan Howard was there, Jimmy Gateley, all the guys in your band.

"These people came up to us backstage and said, 'We'll feed you guys a big steak dinner if you'll come out to our place when the show's over. We'll sneak you in the back door and

Porter Wagoner

Porter Wagoner laughs when he tells the story of once going inside the walls of the Tennessee State Penitentiary to film a video for his classic recording, "Green Green Grass Of Home."

"At the end of the day when we had finished filming," he smiles, "some of the prison officials came up and told me that several of the inmates wanted to meet me. They asked if it would be all right.

"I told them, 'Sure,' and eight or ten of the guys stepped up and shook my hand. Back near the end of the line was this ole boy the guards said was the clown of the group. They told me he had been in jail for 21 years.

"Well, when this guy got up to where I was standing he never said a word. He just looked me up and down a couple of times, stepped back and said, 'Hell, if this is what people look like on the outside these days, I'd rather stay in here!'"

nobody will even know you are there. You can relax and eat in peace and be on your way. Nobody will even have to sign an autograph. We promise.' We had been eating truck stop hamburgers for days and a steak dinner sounded almost too good to believe. So we piled in the busses and drove out.

"When we got there, they seated us at this big, long table. They had a local band playing, but just as soon as we all got comfortable, the band stopped and these people who had promised us a nice, quiet evening got up on the p.a. system and started announcing to the crowd who all was there. They turned a big ole spotlight on us and told us to stand up when they called our names. Boy, were you mad!"

I remembered by this point in the story, and Narvel was right. I had gotten mad. But hearing about it twenty years later, it cracked me up and I began to roar with laughter. But I had forgotten the punch line.

"When we sat back down to eat," Narvel reminded me, "our steak dinners turned out to be a tray of baloney sandwiches!"

◆

Open access to backstage areas often caused a few problems, as you might suspect. Would-be songwriters, singers, and promoters would find the stars and pester them to listen to "just one song" or to "this great new girl singer I've found." (I fully expect to be delayed at the Pearly Gates someday while St. Peter sings me a song he's just written or hypes me on a new girl singer who has just checked in!) And if there was a "town character" anywhere close by, you could always bet he'd show up backstage.

There was an ole boy who lived around Columbus, Ohio, named Roger, and anytime we were within a hundred miles of his home, he'd be at the show. But I'll bet he never bought a ticket in his life. He didn't have to. He seemed always to be able to finagle his way backstage.

He even had himself a badge made that read, "America's No. 1 Country Music Fan," and I never saw him without it pinned to his shirt or sweater. He seemed to be a pretty nice guy, about a half-bubble off plum, maybe, but in a totally harmless way.

One night my band and I were in Columbus with a night off prior to working at a nearby Air Force base the next day. Searching for something to do to pass the time, I thumbed through the local newspaper and discovered Buck Owens was in town for a concert that night at the Veterans Auditorium. I had played at the Vets many times (I would later play one of the most infamous shows of my career in that building, but I'll save that story) and I figured it might be fun to take all the guys and go down and listen to Buck. It was the mid-sixties, Buck was the hottest act in country music, and the show was a sellout.

"Don't worry about that," I told the group, "we can get in the stage door. I know all those guys. No problem." So we climbed aboard our bus and drove to the show.

When we parked and walked as a group to the stage entrance, I realized almost immediately that I had vastly underestimated the power of a Buck Owens concert. There were security guards everywhere. Recently hung "Positively No Admittance" signs screamed from every possible entrance to the building. I still felt sure I could get us in, but perhaps I was going to have to pull a few more strings than I had originally planned.

I walked up to the guard who was standing outside the stage entrance I had used many times when working that same building myself. I stuck out my hand and said, "Hi, I'm Bill Anderson." His eyes never blinked. They glared back, cold as icicles.

President Richard Nixon came to Nashville for the opening of the new Grand Ole Opry house in March, 1974. He watched part of the show from the audience and then came on stage with Roy Acuff. The two of them toyed with Roy's trademark yo-yo, the President got in several humorous ad libs, and then he sat at the Opry piano and led the audience in singing "God Bless America."

When the President's stint on stage was over, he left the building and it was back to Opry business as usual. Jan Howard was the next artist scheduled to perform. Understandably, she wasn't too thrilled about it.

"I've had some tough acts to follow in my career," she told the crowd, "but I wouldn't give this spot to a dry cleaner!"

"Bill Anderson," I repeated. "Grand Ole Opry. Nashville. I've performed here many times. Don't guess we've ever met. Nice to meet you, though."

Nothing.

"Uh, this is my band, and we're all friends of Buck and his band, and we'd like to stick our heads in the door and say hello. OK?"

"You got a pass?"

"Well, uh, no . . . ."

"Nobody gets in here without a pass."

"But we're friends and I . . . ."

"Look, pal, I said nobody . . . ."

I could tell I was getting nowhere fast. I was planning my next move when suddenly, up over the guard's left shoulder, something caught my eye. I strained to get a closer look. When I did, I saw standing there at the top of a small flight of stairs leading to the dressing room area backstage a face I had seen many times. And below the face, a badge I had memorized.

"Hey," I snapped at the guard. "How did he get in there?"

"Oh, he's America's No. 1 Country Music Fan," the guard answered defensively. Like, "Hey, he's *somebody*! What did you say your name was again?"

From his perch at the top of the stairs, America's No. 1 Country Music Fan called down to the guard, "It's OK, officer. They're friends of mine. You can let them in."

And that's how Bill Anderson got in to see Buck Owens.

Honest.

The Grand Ole Opry's Sam McGee, shaking his head and looking forlornly at his own banjo after having heard the great Earl Scruggs pick the banjo for the first time:

"I think I'll take mine home and build a hen's nest in it!"

CHAPTER SIX

If package shows with big stars and big crowds in nice auditoriums in major cities had been all we played in my early days in the music business, life would have been pretty smooth. And pretty boring. For one thing, I wouldn't be sitting here now writing about the time I shared not only the stage but a dressing room with a stripper.

In the early sixties, if you wanted to sing country music for a country music audience in Kansas City, Missouri, you got yourself booked into a small, smoky tavern on the east side of downtown called Genova's Chestnut Inn. Package shows came to Kansas City, of course, but normally they played the auditorium across the river on the Kansas side.

Charlie Genova, who owned and managed the Chestnut Inn, looked as though he came right out of every black and white gangster movie you ever saw. Central casting would have loved him—the bad guy, the head of the gang, the short, fat Italian who sat in his easy chair puffing on a big cigar, barking orders to his underlings.

Charlie ran every facet of the Chestnut Inn, booked in all the country acts, and yet I doubt seriously if he knew Andy Williams from Hank Williams. Nor do I think he cared. The only music important to Charlie Genova was the tune the customers played on the keys of his cash register.

And he knew how to make those keys ring like a symphony. His methodology was a bit unorthodox, perhaps, but the results were undeniable. For it was he who came up with the idea of booking male country singing stars onto the same bill with female strip-tease dancers. And in the Chestnut Inn, for awhile at least, it worked.

I indicated in the beginning that this book would not stoop to the level of a supermarket tabloid in detailing the off-stage exploits of country entertainers. At the same time, everybody knows the stars of our music are not choirboys. Two separate incidents from the past illustrate that fact, at the same time providing humorous insight into the quick and fertile minds possessed by a pair of our finest.

Both stories involve married male country singing stars who hosted parties in their hotel rooms following a concert. In each case, the liquor flowed freely and members of the opposite sex abounded.

At one party, the star carelessly allowed someone with a Polaroid camera to snap his picture as he reclined in a rather compromising pose with an attractive young lady. Without anyone's noticing, the photographer casually flipped the print aside. Nobody saw it land in the singer's suitcase where it lay undisturbed for the remainder of the tour. The first person to see the picture was the star's wife when he returned home and she unpacked his luggage.

Confused and angered by what she saw, the wife snatched the picture out of the suitcase and defiantly confronted her husband. "Would you like to explain this?" she asked.

She was no match for the mental agility of her mate. "Yes, darling," he said as he studied the picture for the first time and raced to find a plausible explanation. "I brought that home for you to see. Just look at it. Isn't it amazing how much that man looks like me?"

◆

A t the other party, our hero ran short of liquor somewhere in the wee hours and sent the hotel bellman out to fetch another supply. While waiting for his return, the star lounged comfortably with the chosen lady of his fancy in nothing but his under - shorts and cowboy boots. Suddenly there came a knock on the door.

Assuming it to be the bellman returning with the refreshments, the star made no effort to hide his mostly-naked body nor his indiscretion. He marched to the door and flung it open. To his total astonishment, however, it was not the bellman with the booze. It was, instead, the singing star's wife.

Again, this being a man of swift wit and rapid recovery, the star turned a most memorable line:

"Well," he snapped before his wife could utter even a word, "are you gonna believe what you see or what I tell you?"

I say it worked. It worked as far as packing the joint with people every night was concerned. From an artistic point of view, it left more than a little to be desired.

I hadn't been on stage ten minutes my first night there when the male natives who had gathered around the bar began to grow restless. They gripped their beer bottles tightly around the necks and started banging the

Roy Clark:

"You can tell at an early age when your kid is gonna be in the music business. You catch him teething on a thumb pick."

bottoms down loudly on the counter. "Bring on the girls!" they chanted in unison. It was obvious they had not been lured to the Chestnut Inn in anticipation of hearing me whisper.

On the other hand, a group of ladies seated at tables across the room evidently *had* come for the music, and they began saying, "Ssshhh—we want to hear Bill!" back at the guys. The battle was on. And there I stood, in the middle of a small wooden square that had once been a dance floor but which now served as a stage, attempting to perform through the crossfire.

I honestly do not remember the stripper's name who was on the bill with me. In fact, I don't remember either of her names, her real name or whatever it was that she called herself when she took off her clothes. What I do remember is finally coming off stage and walking into Charlie Genova's office (which doubled as my dressing room, the stripper's dressing room, and Charlie's lounge for watching TV) after my emotionally-draining first set and seeing this lady calmly seated in front of her make-up mirror in what might most charitably be described as a rather provocative stage of undress.

She had not arrived at the club prior to my first show. I had changed my clothes in privacy, and I hadn't even met her. I stood in the doorway thinking she might acknowledge my presence or someone might introduce us in a minute, but Charlie was the only other soul in the room and he wasn't paying either one of us a bit of attention. I decided to just stay cool and pretend she was my sister. But that wasn't easy either. I mean, the lady had obviously been driven hard and put up wet a few times in her life. She did not look like the sisterly type!

On the other hand, she was not what you would call ugly by a long shot. But in all that I had learned from the superstars of country music on the package show tours, no one had ever bothered to pull me aside and tell me what you're supposed to say when you walk into your dressing room and find a naked lady seated there. I thought of, "Hi," but somehow that just didn't seem to quite cut it.

She began to put on whatever it was she was putting on so that she could go on stage and take it off again, and continued to ignore me completely. I guess

I was once approached by a company wanting to sponsor my television show in over 100 markets—provided I would personally deliver their commercial messages. The potential for exposing my music to such a wide audience excited me, but there was a catch: The would-be sponsor manufactured tombstones.

As much as I wanted the exposure for my music, I wasn't real sure I wanted to do commercials for tombstones. I finally turned down the offer when someone showed me the opening line of the commercial they wanted me to present:

"If you loved them when they were here," it read, "you'll want to be able to find them when they're gone!"

I wasn't her type. Either that, or tall guys dressed in black rhinestone cowboy suits and carrying a guitar popped into her dressing room all the time. I sighed, and slid my D-45 Martin calmly back into its case.

She finished dressing and slithered out the doorway and onto the stage to the accompaniment of loud cheers from the men who had been waiting for her and muffled titters of feigned embarrassment from the women who had come to hear me sing. It was then, as the dressing room door closed behind her and I stood alone in the middle of the room, that I realized I had not yet spoken to Charlie Genova.

Fact was, he hadn't even looked my way the whole time I had been in the room. His attention was riveted instead on a twelve-inch, black and white console television set standing in the corner of the room. He was seated in a padded easy chair facing the TV, leaning back ever so slightly, his unlighted cigar clinched tightly between his teeth. His hands lay crossed on top of his ample stomach, rising and falling with each breath he took.

From the TV I heard the word, "Ness." I looked up just in time to catch a glimpse of Robert Stack climbing into a car and being sped away. I realized Charlie was watching "The Untouchables," the story of crime-fighter Elliot Ness and one of the top-rated TV shows of the day. But Charlie, as I came to learn, wasn't just *watching* the show, he was *in* the show. The good guys were in their cars chasing the bad guys through the streets of Chicago and bullets were flying everywhere and Charlie Genova was sitting there in his tiny office-cum-dressing-room-for-a-hillbilly-singer-and-a-stripper *rooting* for the bad guys. Every time the black hats would turn a corner in their car without having gotten blown away, he would cheer. Not cheer as in, "rah-rah for ole Notre Dame," but he'd breathe a noticeable sigh of relief and let out a low, soft moan.

I mean, the whole scene was right out of the funny papers. Strip-tease dancer on stage taking off her clothes, men whistling and yelling, women hiding or pretending to hide their faces, cash register jingling like Roy Rogers'

A well-known country singer once met a young girl at a concert and invited her to his hotel room after the show.

She met him there, and in no time at all found herself lying across his bed, wrapped in his arms. As things began to grow even more intimate the young girl panicked.

"I can't," she suddenly exclaimed and jumped up from the bed.

"What's the matter?" the singing star asked.

"I've never done anything like this before," she cried.

The singer was taken back and suddenly began to feel guilty. After all, he reasoned, the girl was rather young. He rose from the bed and began to apologize. He helped her gather her belongings and gently walked her to the door.

"I'm really sorry," he said. "I had no idea you had never done this before." And he opened the door.

Realizing she was about to lose the only chance she might ever have to be with her idol, the young lady suddenly had a change of heart.

"Wait a minute," she cried. "I just remembered. There was this one time . . . ."

spurs at roundup time, hillbilly singer from Tennessee standing quietly in his black rhinestone suit watching crazed Italians whoop it up one more time for Al Capone. If video cameras had been invented, I'd have won the hundred-thousand dollar prize on "America's Funniest Videos!"

Pretty soon "The Untouchables" went off TV, the news came on, Charlie Genova lost interest, and the stripper came back to the dressing room, breathing hard and perspiring from every pore of her body . . . and I could see most all of them!

"Your turn," she whispered to me as she reached for a towel. I jumped back, not sure I wanted a turn. Then I realized she meant it was my turn to go back out on stage and face the natives. Charlie Genova wasn't big on intermissions.

I found out quickly that it was one thing to precede a stripper on stage, quite another to follow one. By the start of my second set, the audience was completely out of control. The men at the bar were mostly very drunk, very loud, and very obnoxious. The women were mad at the men because they wouldn't shut up. They were also mad at the stripper because she looked better than most of them. And the men were upset because they had to listen to me sing before they could see the stripper again. And the women were still mad at Charlie Genova for booking the stripper onto a country music show in the first place. I cautiously eased my way back out onto the battlefield, only to be provided with one of the more memorable lines of my career.

"Hey, Bill, sing 'Walk Out Backwards'," yelled one of the women as I was strapping on my guitar.

"Yeah," chimed in another, "sing 'Walk Out Backwards'. I heard it on the radio today!"

My new record, "Walk Out Backwards (And I'll Think You're Walking In)," had just been released as a single, and this was the first time I had gotten any requests for it. I knew the country station in town had begun to play it, but with most new records you have to wait awhile for the fans to hear it and begin asking for it. I took these requests to be an early indication of a hit, and I got excited. I turned to the leader of the house band, told him to hit me an F-chord, and we took off. When the song was over, the women applauded generously and most of the men yawned. Just as the applause died, however, one ole boy over at the bar yelled out:

"Hey, Bill! That was pretty good! You sing that song a helluva lot better'n that guy on the record!"

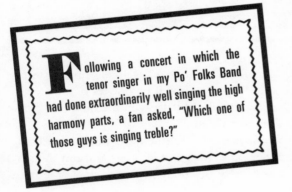

Following a concert in which the tenor singer in my Po' Folks Band had done extraordinarily well singing the high harmony parts, a fan asked, "Which one of those guys is singing treble?"

CHAPTER SEVEN

I got the idea to write "Walk Out Backwards (And I'll Think You're Walking In)" one day when I walked into the kitchen of my small Nashville apartment just as my wife was walking out with two big sacks of garbage. She had a bag in each hand and was pushing open the door with her backside. For an instant, it looked to me as if she were bringing the garbage into the house. She was walking out backwards, but I had thought she was walking in.

I told her how the situation had looked to me and we had a good laugh. Then, as only a songwriter would do, I added, "Hey, that's a good idea for a song. A guy doesn't want his lady to leave him, but he knows she is going to leave anyhow. So he tells her it will be less painful for him if she'll just walk out backwards and let him pretend she's coming in." Like most good songs, from that point on it almost wrote itself.

In the days when I first began to write songs, country songwriters very seldom tried to be cute or clever with their lyrics. Down through the years, most country songs had been about as subtle as a blow to the head with an iron skillet. In fact, country music was known for its straight-ahead, no-frills approach to life:

> *"Whiskey and blood ran together*
> *And I didn't hear nobody pray . . . ."*

or

"I'm driving nails in my coffin
Every time I drink a bottle of booze . . . ."

Country writers never wasted a whole lot of time beating around the bush with songs about moon, spoon, and June.

That's part of what attracted me to country music in the first place. The realism. The honesty. I might not have been old enough to fully understand all the adult ramifications of some of Hank Williams' music, but when ole Hank sang,

"Today I passed you on the street
And my heart fell at your feet . . ."

I knew exactly what he meant. Nobody had to paint me a picture. Hank had painted it with the words to his song.

If my generation of country songwriters in the early to mid-sixties brought anything new to country music, I think it was our approach to lyrics. We wrote straight-on, plaintive songs, but we didn't mind playing with words a bit along the way. Like Roger Miller's "The Last Word In Lonesome Is Me" and "I've Got Half A Mind To Leave You (But Only Half The Heart To Go)."

I'm not saying our generation invented the play-on-words genre of country songcrafting, because we didn't. In the fifties, Marvin Rainwater and Faron Young wrote, "I Miss You Already (And You're Not Even Gone)." Before that,

In the seventies, country music went through an era of what those of us in the business referred to as "skin songs"—a time when it seemed the lyrics to every hit song had to do with warm, tender bodies and soft, sexy skin.

From out of nowhere and right into the midst of this seemingly endless stream of love songs suddenly came the late Red Sovine with a hit recitation about a truck, a truck driver, and a child.

Justifiably proud of his father's accomplishment, Red's son, Roger, boasted to some friends one day, "My dad has a No. 1 record, and it doesn't have anything whatsoever to do with sex!"

"Yes it does," someone replied. "That company he records for is gonna screw him out of all his royalties!"

I remember a Lonzo and Oscar novelty tune called, "You Blacked My Blue Eyes Once Too Often." And there were others. We simply took the form and expanded on it.

Too, we didn't try to write clever songs nearly so much as we tried to write "hook lines," distinctive little phrases or thoughts that would jump out of a song and defy the listener to forget them. There have been some great hook lines in country songs over the years:

"The worst you ever gave me was the best I ever had."

"Our marriage was a failure and our divorce ain't workin' either."

"If fingerprints showed up on skin, whose would I find on you?"

"The girl who waits on tables used to wait for me at home."

"I turned out to be the only hell my mama ever raised."

"It was always so easy to find an unhappy woman 'til I started looking for mine."

"She's just a name dropper, and now she's droppin' mine."

"I've got you on my conscience, but at least you're off my back."

"Lord, I need somebody bad tonight, 'cause I just lost somebody good."

"How much more can she stand and still stand by me?"

"God please forgive me—I don't think her husband will."

"I'm gonna put a bar in my car and drive myself to drink."

"If you want to keep the beer real cold, put it next to my ex-wife's heart."

"It takes me all night long to do what I used to do all night long."

"If someone that loves me could hurt me this bad, just think what a stranger could do."

"My wife ran off with my best friend, and I sure do miss him."

"Get your tongue out of my mouth, I'm kissing you goodbye."

And Roger Miller's classic, "If I can't be your number one, then number two on you."

◆

Those of us in country music have taken a lot of flak over the years regarding the lyrics to some of our songs. My contention is that country song lyrics are

---

Members of the Nashville Songwriters Association were discussing potential candidates for the Association's Hall of Fame when the name of a well known songwriter came up.

"But he didn't write a lot of the songs he is credited with having written," someone said. "He bought them from someone else."

"Yeah, but look at how many monster hits he had," another countered.

To which veteran songwriter Danny Dill interjected, "Maybe the Hall of Fame should start a new category—He Knew A Good Song When He Heard One!"

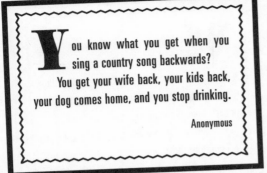

like anchovies: Some people like them, some people hate them, but hardly anybody ignores them.

Every so often a major magazine or newspaper will print a list of the best (or worst, depending on your point of view) country song titles and lines from country songs. For months after their publication people quote them. Preachers even use them in their sermons. In fact, I was flipping the TV channels not long ago and heard the Rev. Billy Graham refer to "Walk Out Backwards (And I'll Think You're Walking In)" during one of his crusades. My song, "It's My Life (I'll Throw It Away If I Want To)" provided fodder for many pastoral dissertations when it was at its peak. Several of my other compositions invariably show up when people discuss country song titles, among them "I Don't Love You Anymore (Trouble Is I Don't Love You Any Less)," and a song called "Quits."

The line they most often point to from "Quits" is, "We called it magic/ Then we called it tragic/ Finally we called it quits." They make fun of it, but when I wrote that song I said exactly what I wanted to say, just the way I wanted to say it.

The song was inspired by the punch line from an old joke. I used to introduce my drummer, Snuffy Miller, on stage as "Quits Miller." I said, "When his parents were expecting him, they couldn't decide on a name. After he was born, his dad took one look at him and said to his mother, 'Let's call it quits.'"

Riding down the road one night I began to apply that thought to a male-female relationship that had started off beautifully but had ended up going sour: "We couldn't call it happy though it was for awhile/ We couldn't call it sad 'cause it taught us both to smile/ We ran out of anything to call it, so we called it quits." I thought it was a plain, forthright assessment of a sad situation. The fact that it also happened to be a semi-clever play on words was simply the icing on the cake.

◆

I have several favorite country music song titles and hook lines, and I'm constantly on the lookout for new ones. One of the best was sent to me in the mail when I put out the word that I was looking for a song for a friend of mine who was about to cut his first record.

"Tell me something about the guy," the writers would all say. "What's he like? What kind of song does he want to sing?"

How do you describe a singer no one has ever heard? "Well, he's been married and divorced three times," I said. "And he has a marvelous sense of humor. Does that help?"

A young singing hopeful, in Nashville to cut his first phonograph record, walked confidently into a major publishing company looking for songs he might possibly record. He told the song-plugger in charge:
"Play me everything you have in the key of D!"

A few days later, Billy Edd Wheeler and Steve Clark, who between them have written such monster hits as "Coward Of The County" and "I'd Be Better Off In A Pine Box (On A Slow Train Back To Georgia)" sent me a song for my friend to record. It was called, "I Hope You're Livin' As High On The Hog As The Pig You Turned Out To Be."

I flipped out. I ran to my friend exclaiming, "I have found you the perfect country song! It's the story of your life set to music!" He took one look at the title and said, "I pass."

Country songs sometimes have a way of hitting folks a little too close to home.

◈

Years ago, a would-be songwriter called my mom and dad at home in Georgia saying he desperately needed to know how to get in touch with me in Nashville.

"I've written a hit song for Bill," this person exclaimed. "I know he'll just love it. It's called, "I'm Pea-Green With Envy And Blue Over You.""

Don't bother searching my greatest hits catalog. It's not in there.

◈

Amateur songwriters often go to extreme lengths to get the attention of someone they think can help them get their songs recorded. I was at Tree Publishing one day when the mailman brought in a Special Delivery package for Buddy Killen. On the outside was stamped in big red letters: "THIS

I once received a fan letter addressed to my syndicated television show:
"On next week's program, please have Bill Anderson sing 'The Tips Of My Fingers' in the key of C, vocal with instrumental accompaniment."

There was a time during his illustrious career that the great Tex Ritter did not carry a full band with him on tour. He would fly to most of his concert appearances and have the promoter of the show furnish him with a back-up band when he arrived.

One day a promoter had picked up Tex at the local airport and was driving him to the venue. Along the way, he began to boast about the band he had secured for Tex.

"You're really going to love these guys, Tex," he predicted. "They've got a super guitar player."

Tex didn't say a word, just puffed on his pipe and stared out the window.

"And the drummer is terrific, too," the promoter went on. "And the bass player."

Tex continued to ride in silence.

Finally the promoter added, "And this band has a great accordion player!"

That got Tex's attention. He took his pipe out of his mouth, turned to the driver and said firmly, "Sir, there is no such thing as a great accordion player!"

Tex Ritter

PACKAGE CONTAINS ANOTHER HIT SONG FROM THE WRITER OF 'PLEASE PASS THE COOKIES, MOTHER.'"

◆

Connie Smith once received a song in the mail entitled "Thank God For Bill Anderson Because He Discovered Connie Smith."

And the writer wanted *Connie* to record it!

◆

A woman sent me a tape of a song she wrote but which, she said, "should be sung by a man. I don't have one right now, though," she admitted, "so I'll sing it myself."

◆

Music publisher Terry Choate swears he once was sent a song called "The California Hot Tub Rectal Gonorrhea Blues." Johnny Horton's former manager, Tillman Franks, found one called "The Only Good Years We Had Were The

Funnyman Johnny Russell toured with Charley Pride for several years, opening Charley's shows and serving as his good-natured sidekick and travelling companion. Over a period of time, Johnny came to know Charley's personality and delighted in needling him.

Once during Johnny's tenure with the show, Charley, who, of course, was country music's first black superstar, hired a black saxophone player for his band. Up to that point, all Charley's travelling musicians and backup singers had been white. When the new man joined the band, Johnny immediately began to heckle him.

Johnny Russell and Bill

One day during rehearsals, Charley picked up on the razzing and called Johnny aside.

"Hey, man, how come you're on my new guy's back all the time? Are you prejudiced or something?"

"Heck, yeah, I'm prejudiced," Johnny answered.

"You don't like blacks?" Charley asked defensively.

"Naw," Johnny replied. "I don't like saxophone players!"

Tires On Our Car," and another titled "If Things Don't Start Picking Up, I'm Gonna Start Picking Up Things." Songwriter/publisher Dav、 Lindsay still laughs over a song he was mailed, "Thank God For Runaway Truck Ramps." In 1959, Johnny Cash received a demo, complete with sound effects, called "The Mating Of The Monster And The Hag." A well-worn Music Row tape from the sixties was titled, "If Your Hair's Too Long There's Sin In Your Heart." And I had a masterpiece called "Only Dumb Girls Get Pregnant" delivered in person by its creator to a recording studio one afternoon just prior to one of my sessions.

As the title implies, it was an ode to birth control, written and sung by a middle-aged lady who could neither write nor sing. She not only played the piano badly and warbled in graphic, falsetto, out-of-tune detail on how to prevent babies, but she charged into a chorus on feminine hygiene as well. When it wasn't piercing my eardrums, it was turning my stomach.

I kept her tape, however. Someday one of the "rap" artists will probably record it and have a No. 1 smash!

The worst song *title* I ever saw came in the mail, unsolicited, of course, from an amateur songwriter. I never listened to the song. I figured the title was bad enough. I don't believe the writer was trying to be sacrilegious, though, because I'm told the song itself was actually written in a positive vein.

But it was called, "There Ain't No Flies on Jesus."

And there is, of course, no truth whatsoever to the rumor that country hunk Billy Ray Cyrus has a song coming out entitled "There Ain't Enough Room In My Fruit of the Looms To Hold All My Love For You."

The humor in these next three stories may be lost on those outside the music business—the normals. We abnormals think they are funny:

It seems that an angry band of Indians once had a small Cavalry regiment completely surrounded and were poised to attack. The pulsating sound of war drums began to echo across the valley. Softly at first, then louder. Louder. The soldiers grew fearful.

"I don't like the sound of those drums," a frightened young cavalryman said to the officer at his side.

Whereupon the Indians yelled back defensively, "He's not our regular drummer!"

A musician was telling a fellow musician about a terrible band he had recently heard.

"The steel player was so flat," he said, "even the fiddle player noticed!"

And then there was this line from a news report on an automobile accident involving a travelling band:

"Injured in the wreck were three musicians and a drummer."

You didn't laugh? Just proves you are normal.

CHAPTER EIGHT

I liked working the big package show tours with all the great artists of the day, but there were none I enjoyed more than the tours I worked with Johnny Cash.

For one thing, when John was headlining the show, I always knew we would be playing to big crowds. He was the superstar of all superstars. And he surrounded himself with such a dynamic cast:

Johnny Western to open the shows and serve as master of ceremonies; Gordon Terry to sing and show off on the fiddle; the Carter family to bring forth the old mountain ballads then step aside and sing background harmonies; June Carter (later Mrs. June Carter Cash) to play comedy and sing duets with John. When I tagged along, it was as a special featured guest.

Of course, John always had his band in tow, the Tennessee Three. In later years he would expand to a larger group, but in those days the music that came from Luther Perkins on guitar, Marshall Grant on bass, and W.S. "Fluke" Holland on drums was music aplenty. Anything else would have cluttered the sparse but dynamic arrangements the people had come to expect from having heard John's recordings.

Johnny Cash may have never known it, and even if he did I'm sure he's forgotten it by now, but he was once responsible for my not quitting the music business.

I hadn't been in Nashville long and I wasn't making very much money. I had written a successful song or two and a couple of my own recordings had darted in and out of the charts, but very little of that was translating into bookings for personal appearances. And in those days, with the biggest country record hits selling only fifty thousand or so copies, if you didn't work the road you didn't eat.

My vote for the coolest line ever spoken by someone in the country music business goes to a veteran Los Angeles radio personality, the late Dick Haynes. Unfortunately, it came at a time when his microphone wasn't even open.

It was the morning of the giant earthquake that rocked southern California in the early seventies. Haynes, who had delighted tens of thousands of listeners with country music and country humor every day for years, was broadcasting from K-FOX, whose studios were on the fourteenth floor of a new cylinder-shaped office tower only a few yards from the ocean at Long Beach. He and the morning newsman were the only two people in the building when the quake began to rumble beneath the ground.

The building started to vibrate and shake violently. Phonograph records came tumbling out of the record bins and spinning across the floor. Rolls of recording tape were plummeting everywhere, microphones were wavering, phonograph needles were jumping in and out of the grooves of the records the station was attempting to broadcast. The young news reporter dropped everything and ran into Haynes' control room totally terrified.

"Oh, my God," he cried to the veteran announcer. "It's an earthquake! How do we get outside?"

Haynes never looked up. He simply replied, "Dial nine."

I was newly married. My rent had skyrocketed from the fifty-five dollars a month I paid to the landlord who owned the tiny cabin where I lived when I first moved to town all the way up to eighty-five dollars a month for the one-bedroom upstairs apartment I had found for me and my new bride. Groceries had more than doubled, from eleven-dollars my first week in town up to nearly twenty-five. And I still hadn't been able to talk Ma Bell into sending back my hundred dollar deposit on the telephone. As most entertainers eventually do, I was paying my dues.

I remember the night well. My wife and I had been sitting around since dinner trying to decide about our future. Did we want to admit this music business thing had been a big mistake and go back home to Georgia, where I felt certain I could get a job at a radio station somewhere, and give up this glamorous but crazy dream? Or did we want to try to ride it out a bit longer and see what lay around the next bend in the road? We could come up with good reasons for going and good reasons for staying. What were we supposed to do? We couldn't make up our minds and it was getting late. We decided to turn in, sleep on it, and talk some more in the morning.

Just as we were getting ready for bed, the telephone rang. It was nearly midnight. Neither of us could imagine who might possibly be calling at that late hour. I picked up the receiver, almost expecting the worst.

"Hello."

"Bill Anderson, please," a voice said on the other end of the line.

"This is he," I answered, not recognizing the caller at first.

"Bill, this is Stu Carnall in California," he said. "How are you doing?"

I couldn't believe my ears. Stu Carnall? *The* Stu Carnall? Manager of Johnny Cash? Calling me at home in the middle of the night? Was this some kind of joke?

I wasn't about to say, "Oh, glad you called Stu. I was just in the process of quitting the music business." So I simply lied and told him I was doing fine.

"Well, I've got something I thought you might be interested in," he continued. "John has a four-day tour coming up in Michigan and we need somebody to work the dates with us. I checked and your new record's doing real well up there. I thought maybe you'd like to go up and work with us."

I love small towns and the wonderfully innocent ways in which small-town people often approach big-time situations. For example, I once arrived for a concert in a small northeastern community to find posters in the windows of all the major stores announcing our show. The posters read:

COMING IN PERSON:

**BILL ANDERSON
JAN HOWARD
JIMMY GATELEY**

AND

THREE MORE

And down at the bottom of the poster where you might expect the find ticket information it read:

**IF YOU WOULD LIKE TO ATTEND,
SEE SAM THE POLICEMAN.
HE HAS THE TICKETS.**

We laughed, then were totally shocked the next night when the auditorium was packed to the rafters.

I was speechless. "Can't pay you much," he went on, "just a hundred bucks a day. But I thought we might have some fun."

Not much? "Just" a hundred bucks a day? Good grief, when I left Georgia I was making fifty dollars a *week* at the radio station. A hundred bucks a day for four days would pay my rent for four months with some left over. Somebody Up There obviously wasn't too thrilled with my thinking about giving up music.

"That's great, Stu. I'll be there. When and where?"

I wrote down the details and never went to sleep all night. If memory serves me correctly, I think I sat up and wrote a song.

The first time I ever saw "The Man In Black" he wasn't wearing black at all. He was dressed in a bright red sportcoat, dark slacks, and two-tone black and white loafers. It was 1958, and he had just sung on stage at the Opry. He still had on his stage clothes and was climbing into the back seat of a taxicab on Fifth Avenue outside the Ryman Auditorium. I could tell he was in a hurry, but I walked up and pulled on his sleeve just the same.

"Johnny, I'm Bill Anderson," I said. "I'm a disc jockey on WJJC radio in Commerce, Georgia. I'm up here as Mr. D.J. USA this week on WSM, and I just wanted to let you know how much I admire you and your music. I wear your records out on my radio shows back home."

Johnny's head and shoulders were already inside the door of the cab, but upon hearing me say that I was a disc jockey, he stopped and pulled himself back out. "It's nice to meet you," he said humbly. "Sorry I'm in such a hurry, but I've got to catch a train to Chicago. Got a show up there tomorrow. Thanks for playing my records." And he climbed back inside the cab and was gone.

I also have very vivid memories of once seeing Johnny Cash dressed completely in white. It was on a Sunday afternoon in Texas, and Johnny, Ernest Tubb, and several others of us were at the city auditorium in San Antonio to do a show for Mrs. Carrie Rodgers, widow of Jimmie Rodgers, the man we all refer to today as having been the father of country music.

Johnny wasn't in good health. It was during the time he was having all the throat problems that eventually interrupted his recording career and he was pale and hoarse. I was standing stage-left in the wings with Mrs. Rodgers, each of us straining to hear what Johnny was saying and singing. He turned toward us, his white tux shining in the spotlight, and dedicated his moving recitation, "The Harp Weaver," to Mrs. Rodgers. He faced her throughout the entire song, affording the audience only a side view of his tired, thin body. At the end of the song, he was so hoarse he could barely whisper. He blew her a kiss and I saw a tear in her eye. That was the last time I ever saw Johnny Cash wear white.

Johnny Cash

I was with Johnny during several of his well-documented escapades in the sixties, many of which he wrote about in his autobiography. I watched the night his entourage dropped water-filled balloons from the top floor of the Pantlind Hotel in Grand Rapids, Michigan, onto the heads of the guests leaving a formal dance in the ballroom below. I was there the day he charged into the jam-packed hotel coffee shop and "shot" Gordon Terry for "running around with my wife!" John used blanks and Gordon's "blood" was catsup, but no one knew that right off. Still, not one person moved to stop John or come to Gordon's aid. It was spooky.

And I was in the same hotel the night a dirty, stray dog followed John off the street and into the lobby through a revolving door.

"Get that awful dog out of here!" the bellman roared.

"Don't you touch my dog," Johnny Cash bellowed right back.

"Oh, Mr. Cash, I'm so sorry. I didn't realize this was your dog. Please accept my apologies."

John, of course, had never seen the dog before in his life. But he and his band members played the scene to the hilt.

They escorted the dog into the elevator and took it up to their suite. There they gave the dog a bath in the bathtub, dried it off, and tucked it into bed. I wasn't there to see what happened next, but the following morning everyone in the hotel was buzzing about the guests on the top floor who, for some strange reason, had ordered two-dozen hamburgers at midnight.

◆

Ask Johnny to recall some of the most embarrassing moments of his illustrious career, and chances are he'll tell you about the time in 1967 when he agreed to appear as a guest on my syndicated television show. He didn't mean to, but he hung himself out to dry. Nice guy that I am, I let him hang there.

To begin with, Johnny did very little television other than big network shows and specials in those days. The syndicated half-hour shows that Porter Wagoner, the Wilburn Brothers, and I hosted each week just could not attract an artist of his stature. But Jan Howard was the featured female vocalist on my show, and Johnny and Jan were very close.

Jan had once worked as a background singer with the Johnny Cash Show and was, in fact, the voice that chimed in, "Mama sang tenor," on John's immortal recording of "Daddy Sang Bass." Jan had been telling me for quite some time that John had told her he would guest on our show, but I didn't really figure he ever would.

Imagine my surprise, then, the night I walked into the studio for a taping and in behind me walked not only Johnny Cash, but June Carter, Mama Maybelle Carter, and Luther Perkins, as well.

"You got room for some guests on your show tonight?" John asked.

"Room? How about the entire half-hour?" I shot back.

And with that, we turned on the cameras and began a totally unrehearsed thirty-minute salute to Johnny Cash, the man and his music.

Most of the time John and I sat on two stools in front of the band and we talked and he sang. We traced his career with anecdotes and bits and pieces of many of his hit songs. Luther plugged his guitar into one of the Po' Boys' amplifiers, Mama Maybelle got her autoharp, June joined in, and we had a ball.

About twenty minutes into the show, the subject of Jan Howard came up in our conversation. I told John I knew he wouldn't have been there that night had it not been for Jan, and I thanked them both. Then I complimented him on the great touring show he always carried on the road.

"Yeah, and you stole one of our people," John said, in a kidding tone of voice.

"That's right," I laughed, "Jan Howard. I brought her over here and taught her how to whisper."

Without thinking how it might sound, Johnny fired back with the first thought that popped into his mind: "Well, you better watch her. She's liable to teach you how to sing!" Before the words were out of his mouth, his face started to fall.

"Oh, Lord, I didn't mean that," he stammered, covering his face and laying his head on my shoulder. He was truly embarrassed. "I was just . . . ." But it was too late. The studio audience had heard him and was roaring with laughter. The members of my band were falling out everywhere. Snuffy Miller slid off the side of his drum stool and onto the floor. The technicians and the cameramen were trying to hold their hands steady and stay on the job, but it wasn't easy. The entire studio was in hysterics. And the more John tried to apologize the worse it got.

I laughed myself, at first, then I decided to just sit there on the stool beside him with raised eyebrows and watch him squirm.

"Can't you cut that out of the tape?" he pleaded. His face was so red by this time that it actually showed red on camera. "All you Bill Anderson friends . . . uh, fans out there, please . . . I was just kidding." But I wouldn't have asked the director to stop that tape for anything.

It wasn't that I was out to embarrass Johnny Cash, but I thought those few moments revealed a very human side to a legend, a side not many people had ever seen. It was a slip-up, and everybody in the world slips up. I knew he hadn't meant anything ugly by what he had said, and I felt sure the viewing audience would realize that as well.

I was right. The show aired just the way it was taped, and there was no negative reaction at all. Except from Johnny. I still tease him about it from time to time, and he still winces.

◆

Johnny's appearance on my TV show was on videotape, and we could have erased it had we wanted to. Had it been live television, however, it would have been an entirely different matter. It would have instantly gone out on the air just the way it happened. On live TV, you get one chance and that's all. Live TV comes with no retakes, no erasers. It's like a trapeze artist flying high above a screaming crowd without the benefit of a safety net below.

In the mid-sixties, a young Grand Ole Opry star from Florida named Bobby Lord hosted a live, hour-long television show every weekday afternoon on WSM-TV in Nashville. It was the top-rated show in town, watched not only by the fans and stars of country music but by a large contingent of normals as well. The exposure from such a show was a tremendous boost to Bobby's career, and he approached superstar status within the station's viewing area. The grueling schedule of his having to be in the studio every day, Monday through Friday, was very taxing, however, and every once in a while, Bobby would need to take a day

Bobby Lord has a marvelous sense of humor and a great eye and ear for a story. And he tells some of the best ones on himself.

Once in the late fifties, when he was a star of the Red Foley Ozark Jubilee television show, he says he arrived in a small town for a concert at the local theater only to find his name mis-spelled on the marquee outside. It read:

In Person Tonight
Direct From The Ozark Jubilee
BABY LARD

off and rest.

One night he called and asked me if I would sit in for him the following afternoon and host the show. I had appeared with him many times as a guest and I was happy to help out. What he didn't tell me, however, was that a high school jazz combo was booked onto the show that particular afternoon.

What I knew about jazz or pop music or any other music outside of country in those days could have been written in hieroglyphics on the side of a guitar pick.

When the young combo arrived for rehearsal, therefore, I was surprised to learn that I had actually heard of one of the songs they were going to play, "Sugar Blues," a tune popularized back in the thirties by Clyde McCoy. I'm not sure I had actually ever heard the song, but I had heard *of* it.

According to the program log the director handed me, the band intended to play another song first, one I was totally unfamiliar with, and then play "Sugar Blues" for their closer. In between, I was supposed to walk over to the leader of the group and interview him briefly.

Everything started out fine. I got the group on camera for their first song with no problem, but while they were playing, the director sent word he wanted to see me in the control room. I left the studio, paying no mind whatsoever to what the band was playing, and went where I had been summoned.

I got back onto the set just as the song ended, out of breath and my mind on whatever it was the director had needed to see me about. I raced over to the band leader and aimlessly began to talk. Where do you guys go to school? How long have you been together? Is this what you want to do after you graduate? All the usual stuff. And then I decided it was time for them to begin playing their second song.

"Folks, the song this fine young group is about to play now is one of my all-time favorites," I lied into the camera. It was simply a title I knew, nothing more. "I've been waiting all day for this tune," I went on, "and I know you'll like it too. Here they are again with the great Clyde McCoy song, 'Sugar Blues'!"

Silence. Dead silence.

"OK, guys, let's hear it . . . the great 'Sugar Blues,'" I prodded. "You're on!"

Silence. More silence. Long, *painful* silence. Finally the leader of the group cleared his throat, looked up at me, and said, "Mr. Anderson, we've already played 'Sugar Blues.' That's the one we played first."

I looked around for a shovel. All I could think of was, "Dig a hole, fool, and crawl in it as quick as you can!"

CHAPTER NINE

I probably got to know Faron Young as well or better than any of the big stars during my early days in Nashville. It helped that he was one of the first major recording acts to be attracted to my Nashville-written songs.

In those days, when an artist was about to go into the studio for a recording session, he or she would make the rounds of the three or four major publishing companies in town to listen to songs. The publishers would pull out the best new material their writers had written and attempt to match the singer with just the right song, convincing the artist in the process that said song was a hit just waiting to be sung.

Not all songwriters, however, liked publishers plugging their songs. Some of the greats like Hank Cochran and Harlan Howard and Roger Miller preferred to pitch their songs directly to the artists themselves. They would hang out backstage at the Opry or across the alley at Tootsie's famed Orchid Lounge with the stars who were about to record and, when they sensed the timing was right, they'd pull out a guitar and begin showing off their newest creations. They got many, many hits recorded that way.

Roger used to say that the best songplugger in the world is the guy who sat up all night and wrote the song. "He wrestled with it," Roger reasoned, "wrestled it to the floor. The next day, he's got it. When he sings you that song, he feels every note of it."

I was just the opposite of Roger. I wanted somebody else to pitch my songs to the artists. I agreed wholeheartedly with his assessment of a writer's being the most qualified person to present his own composition, but I've never been able to promote my own songs very well. Maybe it's because I look at my songs as if they are my children. I created them, gave birth to them, nurtured them. I can't stand the thought of showing my new child to someone and having them say, "Gee, your kid is ugly!" I preferred to let someone else show my children off for me.

Buddy Killen, in trying to get Tree Publishing off the ground in the late fifties, had become one of the best song-pluggers in town. Having been a singer and musician himself, he had a natural "feel" for a good song and an uncanny ability to place just the right song with just the right artist. He was friends with all the major stars. He had gained their confidence and they trusted his judgment. As a result, he ultimately became the most successful music publisher in Nashville.

In the fall of 1959, I had written a couple of new songs, an up-tempo story song called "Riverboat" and a country weeper titled "Face To The Wall," and I had recorded demonstration tapes on both of them with nothing but my guitar in the small studio at Tree. Unbeknownst to me, Buddy had listened to my demos over and over until he knew the songs as well as I did. When Faron Young came by Tree to listen to songs for his upcoming session, Buddy was ready.

He pulled a stool up to the old, cracked, out-of-tune piano that lived in the corner of his office and sang my new compositions for Faron himself. Faron liked them both. He liked them so well, in fact, that he told Buddy he might just record *both* of them—"if you'll give me half of one of 'em." He meant he wanted to be given half the writers' share of royalties on one of the two songs.

"You'll have to talk to the writer," Buddy told him. "I can't give away something that's not mine."

Faron wanted to know who the writer was.

"New guy in town," Buddy said. "He wrote 'City Lights' for Ray Price. His name's Bill Anderson."

Faron was ever the opportunist. He was leaving town in a few days for Springfield, Missouri, to appear on Red Foley's Ozark Jubilee television show, and he asked, "Is that the same Bill Anderson who's doing the Foley show Saturday night?" Buddy told him it was.

Faron got my phone number from Buddy and called me at home. He asked me if I'd like to ride to Springfield with him in his new black Cadillac. "Oh, and by the way," he added, "I like that new song of yours."

"Which one?" I asked him, not sure exactly which tune Buddy might have played for him.

"Oh, I forget the name of it," Faron fibbed. "We'll talk about it on the way to Springfield."

◆

> **L**oretta Lynn, on an overseas tour, after having received an unfavorable review in a London newspaper:
>
> "If I can get my hands on the guy who wrote that, I'll whup him all over the whole state of England!"

We weren't thirty miles up the road when Faron brought up the subject of the song.

"Actually, I liked two of your songs," he confessed, "but I don't think I can record two songs by the same writer.

"Why not?" I asked.

"Aw, there's so many writers in town that are friends of mine, and they write good songs too. If I cut two of yours, then they'll get pissed off and give all their good songs to Webb Pierce."

I laughed.

"But you know, I've been thinking. I *might* just consider recording both of those songs . . . "Riverboat" and "Face To The Wall". . . if you'll give me half writers' on one of them."

I pretended to be surprised by Faron's offer and I sat there without saying anything for quite awhile. Actually, Buddy had told me this might be coming. The approach was nothing new or anything out of the ordinary. Major stars had been greasing their own pocketbooks with similar tactics for years. Faron had once gotten Roy Drusky to give up part of the hit "Alone With You" by promising to help further Roy's career. Webb Pierce had put his name on several of Mel Tillis' early songs using much the same strategy.

But I wasn't sure I liked that game or wanted to play by those rules. I rode along quietly for awhile, not saying anything. Finally, I asked Faron cautiously, "Which song do you want half of?" fearing he would say "Riverboat." I sensed that song was destined to be the bigger hit of the two.

"Oh, I don't know," he stalled. "How about 'Face To The Wall?'"

I breathed a sigh of relief. "Why that one?"

"I think it needs some re-writing," Faron answered. "It's a pretty good song, but I think I can make it better. We got a deal?"

I felt like I was about to put one of my kids up for adoption, but what could I do? A two-sided Faron Young record in those days was about as good as it could get for a country songwriter. I struggled with it a little while longer and finally answered, "Deal." But only half-heartedly.

Faron did record both songs, and Capitol Records released them back to back on the same single record. They were both hits. "Riverboat" made it to No. 1 in the charts and "Face To The Wall" reached the Top Ten. And Faron was truthful about rewriting part of "his" song. He changed one line.

Thanks to the success of both songs, Broadcast Music, Inc., the music licensing firm, presented me two of their coveted BMI Citation of Achievement Awards that fall. Since Faron's name was on "Face To The Wall," he was given an award as well.

As he and I were basking in the applause and the spotlights following us up to the podium of the posh Belle Meade Country Club to accept our awards, "Face To The Wall" was playing on the big speakers placed strategically throughout the room. I turned to Faron and said mockingly, "Great little song you wrote there, Sheriff."

"Anderson, I don't think I'd be complaining if I were you," he shot back.

I assured him I was joking. I was not complaining. I had nothing to complain about at all.

◆

You hang around the music business in Nashville long enough and you'll hear all kinds of stories about Faron Young. Some paint a good picture of the man dubbed "The Young Sheriff" early in his career following a role he played in a western movie, others not so good. Most of the stories are funny, though, because Faron works hard at being one of the industry's true characters. He's also one of country music's very best singers and, when he wants to be, one of the greatest entertainers ever to walk out onto a stage.

In the years following our joint "writing" of "Face To The Wall," I got to know him a lot better and I learned that his asking for half a song is not nearly so much a part of his nature as would be his giving someone the last dime in his pocket. He makes it hard to find sometimes, but underneath all Faron's show-biz fluff and bravado lies a kind, generous human being. Roger Miller may have described him best when he said, "Faron's heart is as big as his mouth!" He and I were neighbors for awhile on Old Hickory Lake. I love him like a brother.

Faron, however, loves to tease me and pick on me. He imitates my soft, breathy voice every chance he gets, and anytime we end up on a radio or television show together, he'll tell about my early days in the business and how I used to become giddy at the sight of one of my records on a juke box. Faron embellishes the story, of course, but that only makes it funnier.

Truth is, it used to thrill me no end every time I would walk into a truck stop or a restaurant or a night club somewhere and actually see one of my own records on the establishment's juke box. To me, that was more exciting, even, than hearing one of my records played on the radio. If the record were on a juke

Faron Young and Bill

box, I reasoned, then the juke box operator had liked it enough to go out and buy a copy of it. And that meant I had made two whole pennies in royalties!

It was easy at first to go into a place with a juke box and stand and search for my own records. Nobody knew who I was. Just some guy looking for some songs to play, right? As I became better known, however, and people began seeing me on television and on stage shows, it became more and more awkward to do what, in the beginning, had seemed so simple.

The late Jimmy Gateley, who worked for me and fronted my Po' Boys band for thirteen years and who also made records himself, had a great description of a carload of hillbillies pulling into a restaurant and easing over to the juke box to examine the lineup of records. He called it "filing by the coffin."

"That's exactly what I feel like when I walk up to a juke box looking for one of my records," he would say, "like I'm a mourner at somebody's funeral, walking by the casket and looking down at the person who died." And he had a point, especially if we "filed by the coffin" and found none of our records looking back at us. When that would happen several times in a row, we'd start wondering if our *careers* had died!

I was once riding in the car with Faron on a string of dates through the midwest and we had stopped for coffee. Faron had gone to the rest room. That could wait as far as I was concerned. As soon as we were shown to our table, I got up to "file by the coffin." The restaurant was packed with people, and

Performers aren't the only ones who are sometimes subjected to criticism from the press. Bobby Smith, who for years was in charge of selling Charley Pride's souvenir items prior to each concert, once received a scathing review in a local newspaper.

Bobby's job with Charlie was to go on stage a half-hour or so before the beginning of each performance and make the audience aware of the Charley Pride mementoes available to be purchased. Charley carried albums, tapes, T-shirts, hats, and assorted paraphernalia like most country artists, and Bobby was a master at inspiring members of the audience to get up from their seats and add some Charley Pride merchandise to their collection.

One newspaper writer took exception to Bobby's colorful, long-winded speech touting Charley's wares, however, and took him to task in the next day's editions. He said Bobby's sales pitch, made in a bright red suit and in a fast-paced, loud tone of voice, cheapened Charley's act. The writer implied that Bobby lacked class.

Charley's manager, Jack Johnson, saw the review the following morning and took Bobby to task. He made it clear that from that point on he expected the pre-show sales pitch to be carried out in better taste.

At the next concert, Bobby showed up at the auditorium wearing a dark business suit and a somber demeanor, absent his usual hoopla. Instead of urging the audience to buy every Charley Pride item in the house, he simply eased on stage, held up one album, and said softly, "I don't guess anybody would want to buy one of these, would you?" Then he turned and walked quietly off stage.

When he reached Jack Johnson, standing in the wings, he paused just long enough to say, "That classy enough for you?" And he kept right on walking.

there's nothing Faron loves better than a big crowd. He came out of the rest room and on his way to the table, spotted me checking out the juke box. It was too much for him to resist.

"Ladies and gentlemen," he bellowed, "may I have your attention please! Please give me your attention!" Knives and forks and spoons clattered against table tops all across the room. People began talking in hushed tones. Who was this little man dressed in coveralls and wearing a baseball cap? And why did he suddenly want their attention? Had something terrible happened?

"Ladies and gentlemen, will you all please look over toward the juke box," Faron continued at the top of his voice. "You see that man standing there?" I looked to see who he was talking about. Suddenly I realized he was talking about me.

"That man's name is Bill Anderson," he yelled, "and he's a new country music singer. He's over there looking to see if he can find any of his own records on that juke box. Bill Anderson, don't forget that name, folks. He really wants to be a big star. Let's give him a hand!" And the whole place erupted into a frenzy. I wanted to crawl inside the juke box and let the needle put me out of my misery.

Faron made his point. From that day on, I began seeking less conspicuous ways to search out the juke boxes. I especially liked the restaurants where each individual booth came equipped with its own juke box menu and speaker. I didn't "file by the coffin" again for a long, long time.

◆

I can never think of Faron Young without remembering our overseas tour together in the seventies.

Faron's recording of "Four In The Morning" had been a big pop hit as well as a country smash, in England. As a result, he had begun to tour the U.K. frequently and had begun to develop quite a large and loyal following. I was thrilled when his British promoter, Jeffrey Kruger, asked if I would like to be Faron's opening act on a two-week tour.

I like England, although I've never been too sure just how they perceive me over there. Two of my biggest American hits, "Still" and "8 x 10," were hits in the U.K. but not by me. A British comedian-singer named Ken Dodd recorded them there, and there was more than a slight difference between his recordings and mine. When he cut those two songs, he did not do the spoken parts as I had done when I recorded them. Instead, he sang both songs in their entirety.

The first time I toured England in the late sixties I, of course, performed both songs the way I had recorded them and had always performed them at home, which meant I sang the choruses and recited the verses. This evidently confused a British newspaper writer who attended one of my concerts and wrote in the London Times:

"Bill Anderson has a curious habit of pausing in the middle of his songs to recite little poems, some of which are so sentimental they would make a greeting card blush."

Conway Twitty was headlining that particular tour, and when he and his band members saw the review they immediately picked up on the "greeting card" line and began calling me "Hallmark." As far as they were concerned, that was my name until we got back home.

◆

Faron and I had a super tour. Our show attracted large crowds and we had a lot of laughs. A two-week tour overseas can become quite exhausting, however, and by the time our last date rolled around, he and I were both tired and more than ready to head for the house. I seem to remember it was his idea.

"Willy, let's fly home on the Concorde," he said one night as we rode the "motor coach" from the concert back to our hotel. "I've done some checking and we can be back in the United States in three hours."

It sounded tempting, but I wasn't sure. Our tickets on a jumbo–jet 747 had been bought and paid for by Mr. Kruger, and it would be only a seven to eight hour flight. We would have to purchase our own tickets on the Concorde.

"Isn't the Concorde awfully expensive?" I asked.

"You cheapskate!" he chided. "You're richer'n ten feet up a cow's ass! What difference does it make how much it costs? We'll be home before that 747 gets off the ground! I'm making our reservations in the morning. You're *going* with me!"

Faron always did have a way with words, especially the salty ones.

CHAPTER TEN

By and large, I have always enjoyed travelling outside the United States, and over the years I've had the pleasure of taking several musicians in my band on their first trips overseas.

Lisa and Laurie Harper, young background singers, had never been out of the country when I scheduled a trip to England. They were excited beyond belief.

"Now, you'll have to take your shots before we go," I jokingly cautioned. They took me seriously.

"What kind of shots do we have to take?" they asked innocently.

"Parvo shots," one of the band members quickly interjected. I suppressed a giggle and played along.

"What's a parvo shot?" the twins wanted to know.

I didn't tell them it was a vaccination shot for animals. I just told them to be sure they each got one prior to the trip. "You can't go to England without having had it," I said as seriously as I could.

They said their doctor looked at them awfully strange when they went to his office and asked to be given parvo shots.

◆

The most fun I ever had with a young musician in regard to travelling outside the United States, though, was the first time I took a young steel guitar player named Sonny Garrish to Canada.

Today Sonny Garrish is one of the top two or three steel players in the world, playing on a high percentage of all the country records out in Nashville.

But he came to town as a member of my band in the mid-sixties, still in his teens and still a bit damp behind the ears.

On this particular tour, we were travelling on my bus, and our schedule called for us to cross from the state of Maine into the Canadian province of New Brunswick about three o'clock in the morning. Riding through the wilderness around one A.M., I decided to have a little fun with Sonny.

"You ever been to Canada before?" I asked, knowing good and well he had not.

"No, sir," he replied.

"You know you have to have shots, don't you?"

"What kind of shots?" he asked nervously.

"I don't know what they're called," I lied, "but let me give you a little advice. When you cross the border, the guards and the doctors and the nurses will all treat you a whole lot better if you're polite to them and if you're dressed real nice." Sonny, like all of us, was travelling through the night in blue jeans and a sweatshirt.

I didn't pursue the conversation, but I could tell he was thinking it over. In a few minutes, Sonny got up from his seat in the front lounge of the bus and retreated to the back.

It was nearly two o'clock when I couldn't stand it any longer. I opened the bulkhead door and found him sitting on the edge of his bunk polishing his shoes. He was freshly shaven, every hair on his head was combed into place, and he was wearing a coat and tie.

"You're not taking any chances I see," I said, trying my best not to laugh out loud.

"No, sir," he answered softly.

When we reached the border I told everyone to stay on the bus while I went inside to check things out. It was nearly three o'clock by this time and the immigration office was deserted. I walked in, introduced myself to the one officer on duty, and told him about our little joke. I asked him if he'd go along. He said sure, it was a slow night, why not.

I retreated to the bus and gathered up the troops. I told Sonny since he was new and didn't have his "papers" that he should walk in first.

"This the man you told me about?" the immigration officer barked when Sonny walked in. I told him, yes, it was.

"You had your shots, boy?" he asked gruffly.

"I was vaccinated once," Sonny replied meekly.

"That won't get it, boy. Sit down."

I handed the officer our immigration papers and he cleared us for entry into Canada. When he finished, he looked at Sonny and said loudly to me, "Nurse won't be here 'til eight o'clock, Mr. Anderson. You'll have to leave this one with me."

"Eight o'clock?" Sonny exclaimed. "How will I get to the show?" We were still a couple of hundred miles from our destination.

"Bus comes by about ten," the officer answered, beginning by now to relish his role in the subterfuge. "Nurse can check you at eight, doctor should be in by nine, you get your shots and catch the bus at ten. Nice to meet you boys. Have a good tour." And he turned and retreated from the room.

I motioned for the band members to go back outside to the bus. I told Sonny I was sorry, but we'd have to go on without him. I had a radio interview first thing in the morning, I lied, and I couldn't miss it. I told him which hotel to come to and assured him we'd be waiting.

We were all on the bus with the motor running when I figured we had punished poor Sonny long enough. I went back inside and confessed my dirty deeds.

It was several days before he spoke to any of us again.

In 1960 I checked into a small motel on the outskirts of Los Angeles only to be told smugly by the mom 'n' pop owners that a movie crew had been on location nearby the week before and several of the stars and cast members had headquartered at this particular motel.

"I'm going to give you Room Three," the lady told me as I filled out my registration form. And she flashed a big, bright smile. I told her room three would be just fine.

"Room Three!" she said again, a bit louder and with more emphasis on the "three" than before. Again I assured her that would suit me just fine.

"ROOM THREE!" she virtually shouted. "Don't you know who stayed in Room Three last week?" I told her I'd just flown in from Nashville and I didn't have any idea.

"Only the star of the movie," she said. "I'm giving you the very room the star used all last week."

"And who was that?" I asked, visions of Marilyn Monroe having slept on my sheets beginning to dance in my head . . . until as serious as could be the lady replied proudly, "Rin Tin Tin!"

CHAPTER ELEVEN

Entertainers, by their very nature, are not your basic, everyday, button-down, double-breasted, business-oriented type of people. If they were, they would probably be accountants or lawyers instead of performers. And they would never end up wandering around places like New York City with pockets or guitar cases full of money.

In the early days, however, the country music business was not nearly as sophisticated as it has now become. Many of our business practices were archaic by today's standards. For example, most of the promoters of our shows back then were not wealthy people, and they didn't have large corporations standing by to underwrite their productions. Quite often the promoter truly lived from hand to mouth. If the show he booked drew a big enough crowd, there was money with which to pay the entertainers. If it didn't, we sometimes had to scratch and shuffle.

For this reason, there was an unwritten law in our jungle—the "Code of the Hillbillies" as it were—that said, "Do not accept a check from a promoter." Our contracts all called for "Payment In Full On Day Of Performance IN CASH." It sounded sensible enough, but even cash sometimes had its drawbacks.

I once had to fly to New York for a photo session at the end of a long Canadian tour that wrapped up on a Sunday night in Vancouver, British Columbia. My flight left long before the banks in Vancouver opened on Monday morning, and when I boarded the plane my pockets were bulging with Canadian cash. I don't remember how much I had, but it was money from the tour and money from souvenir sales combined. It was a lot more money than I had any business carrying around, and I was a nervous wreck all the way to New York.

> **R**oy Acuff was a very wealthy man, but, characteristically, he seldom talked about money at all.
>
> Chet Atkins is credited with this story:
>
> "One time Roy was signing autographs at Opryland, and an ole boy came up to him and said, 'I bet you wish you had a dollar for every one of those you've signed.'
>
> "And Roy replied, 'I have.'"

Nobody mugged me en route, thank goodness, but the very first thing I did after I landed in the Big Apple and checked into my hotel was head for a bank. There were four banks right outside the door of the hotel, one on each corner. I walked to the nearest one.

"I'd like to purchase a Cashier's Check, please," I said to the first available teller.

"Do you have an account here?" she asked.

"No, I'm from out of town and . . . ."

"No Cashier's Checks without an account."

"Wait, you don't understand. I don't want to cash a check. I have cash I want to give you. I need . . . ."

"Sorry, sir. Next."

"Well, that's the most unfriendly place I've ever been in," I thought to myself as I shook my head and walked out the door. "Good thing there are three other banks nearby." I crossed the street and walked into the next one.

I told my same story. "I'd like to purchase a Cashier's Check, please." And I got the same response.

"You got an account with us?"

"Uh, no, but let me explain. You see, I . . . ."

"Nobody gets a Cashier's Check without an account. I'm sorry." I could not believe my ears.

I crossed the street and entered bank number three. This time I decided to introduce myself to the teller first, smile a lot, and turn on some good ole Tennessee sincerity. Maybe that would work. Was it too much to hope that in midtown Manhattan I might even find a country music fan working in a bank?

It must have been, for the third time was not the charm. But this time, when I got turned down, I asked a few extra questions.

"I don't understand *why* you can't take my money," I said.

"We don't know where you got that money," came the reply.

"But I told you. I'm a country music entertainer and I just finished a long tour in Canada and they paid me in cash and . . . ."

"We don't know that. You might have robbed a bank in Toronto for all we know." I hung my head and moved toward bank number four, my last hope. I was starting to *feel* like a bank robber!

It was my final shot and I knew it. If they wouldn't take my money here,

I'd be stuck with it the whole time I was in New York. Sleeping on top of it. Walking down the streets with it hanging out of my socks. Just the thought terrified me.

I decided to really change my tact this time. I strode right past the tellers' cages and asked to see the president of the bank.

"Do you have an account with us?" I heard for the fourth consecutive time.

"Does the president of the bank only see people with accounts here?" I asked. I didn't say so, but I could very easily have been talked into opening an account at that point.

"No, the president of the bank isn't even in. Can someone else help you?"

"Just point me toward the highest ranking official who *is* in," I pleaded. Without a word I was led up a short flight of stairs and introduced to a pleasant enough man wearing glasses, a dark suit, and a red tie.

Jeannie C. Riley laughs when she recalls the Christmas gift she received from her record company the year she released the million-selling "Harper Valley P.T.A."

"I came home from a tour, and sitting in the middle of my living room floor was a color television set exactly like one some friends of mine owned," she says. "I had wanted one like it, and had even gone to the store and priced one not long before. I knew it sold for $300.

"There was a card on it that said, 'Merry Christmas,' and I thought, 'Now that's really a very nice and thoughtful gift.'

"But a few months later when I received my royalty statement, the company had deducted the cost of the TV from my royalties!

"Not only that," she laughs today, "but they charged me $400 for a $300 TV!"

I started from the beginning, speaking slowly, smiling a lot, and praying silently beneath my breath. I had a feeling that by now word had spread all across New York City that there was this Tennessee bumpkin walking up and down Park Avenue begging someone to relieve him of his money. And I knew there were plenty of people in New York City who didn't work in banks who would be more than willing to oblige.

"How do I know you are who you say you are?" Mr. Executive asked. I pulled out my driver's license, voter registration, American Federation of Musicians membership card, two color 8 x 10 color glossies, my latest 45rpm record and an application blank from the Bill Anderson Fan Club. "Don't guess you'd like to join?" I ventured, but my heart wasn't in it.

"What bank do you do business with in Nashville?" he asked, and I told him.

"Well, I'll just call there and check," he said. With that he rose up out of his chair, walked into an adjoining office, and closed the door behind him. In a few minutes he came back out.

"OK, we'll take your cash," he said.

For some reason, I actually said, "Thank you."

He called a teller to join us and we counted out the money and he wrote me the check I had begged for. I thanked him again and got up to leave.

"Wait, not so fast," he said. "There's one more thing."

"What's that?" I asked.

"The money for the phone call to Nashville," he said. "You owe me $5.65."

"You take cash?" I asked, but he didn't even smile. So much for the friendly banks of New York!

That scenario wouldn't have taken place today. For one thing, promoters and entertainers now seldom deal in cash. Most booking agents require the promoter to pay a minimum deposit of half the artist's fee thirty days in advance of the concert. This is usually done by mail or through a bank transfer. If money is exchanged at the concert itself, it's normally done through bank drafts or certified checks, seldom by cash. But years ago, we flew high, wide, and often by the seats of our pants.

I worked a show at an outdoor park in Indiana one Sunday afternoon and went to the promoter's office when the day was winding down to collect my fee.

"I don't have time to stop and pay you right now," the park owner said abruptly. "I'm busy."

"But, I need to head back toward Nashville," I said.

"Look, I said I don't have time right now."

"But, sir, I've done my shows and worked as hard as I could to please you and your crowd, and now I need to get paid and leave." I couldn't remember ever having had anything like this happen before.

The promoter looked disgusted, but he pushed back his chair and sighed, "OK, follow me."

He led me back behind the stage and dressing room area into a small connecting room that appeared to be a combination sitting room and kitchen. In the corner of the room stood an old beat-up refrigerator.

"Back there," he said.

"I beg your pardon?"

"Back there. Behind that refrigerator. Your money's back there."

"Where?" I didn't get it. What was my money doing behind a refrigerator?

"Damn," he muttered, and he reached out his arm and grabbed the back of the refrigerator. With a grinding grunt and a low, mournful groan, he pulled the refrigerator away from the wall. "There," he said, pointing toward the floor.

I looked down into the corner, and there lay the biggest pile of money I had ever seen at one time in one place in my life. One dollar bills, fives, tens, twenties. And on top of the bills and woven throughout the stack were nickels, dimes, quarters, and all manner of change. None of the money was sorted or wrapped or organized in any way. It was just laying there in a big wad.

"What am I supposed to do?" I asked, totally dumfounded by the whole scene.

"Take it," he said.

"How much is there?" I asked.

"Hell, I don't know. And I don't have time to count it. Just take it."

"Wait a minute. I can't take it if I don't know how much is there," I reasoned. "It may not be as much as you owe me."

"It may be *more* than I owe you," he replied impatiently. "Tell you what, I'll make you a deal. You take whatever's there. If it's more than I owe you then you've made a good deal. If it's less, then I guess I've made a good deal."

I looked at the money on the floor, just waiting for me to scoop it up and take it home. I began to realize that it was definitely more than he owed me. Perhaps a *lot* more.

"But I'm not entitled to *more* than you owe me," I said. "And I'm not going to take *less* than you owe me." I was confused, but I was determined.

"You count it out, then," he said, and he turned and walked away.

I stood there for a minute, alone in the room with more money at my feet than the promoter could have owed me for *several* concerts, and all kinds of thoughts running through my head. I knew my best bet was to start raking up the money and run before he got un-busy and changed his mind. At the same time, I was raised being taught that what's mine is mine and what's not mine is somebody else's. And all that money most definitely was not mine.

Finally I got down on my hands and knees and began to count. I counted out exactly the amount I had agreed to work for and stuffed it into my briefcase. There was still a large pile of bills on the floor.

I started for the door, but my curiosity got the best of me. I turned around,

---

When Ferlin Husky resumed touring following open heart surgery, he ordered the first new pair of his trademark white boots that he had ordered in several years.

"I couldn't believe it when I got the bill," he said. "They charged me $365!

"I called the factory and I asked the young man who answered the phone, 'Do you realize the first pair of boots I bought from your company cost me $35?'

"And he said to me, 'Do you realize I wasn't even born then?' Then he went on to explain: 'Mr. Husky, everything has gone up. Materials, labor, everything.'

"I said, 'Yeah, I know, but my foot hasn't gotten any bigger!'"

got back down on my hands and knees and counted the money that remained. It came to more than twice as much as I had counted out for my fee. "Sometimes I wish my mama hadn't raised me to be honest," I thought, and I turned back around and walked out of the room as swiftly as I could.

◆

I wrote this in my autobiography but I think it bears repeating:

I didn't get into the music business because I thought of it as a way to make money. I love what I do so much that I'd do it for free if I could afford to. I've carried a clipping in my wallet for years that reads:

"Find something you like doing so much you'd do it for nothing. Then learn to do it so well that they'll pay you. And you've got it made."

◆

Tammy Wynette once played a show at a political rally in a small northeast Georgia mountain community for a young, aspiring congressional candidate named Zell Miller. When Tammy's show was over, Zell thanked her and handed her a check for $150.

It was early in her career and Tammy Wynette didn't know Zell Miller from Adam. True to the thinking of the day, she feared his check might not be any good. As soon as she left the concert site she drove straight to the nearest bank.

(L-R) Zell Miller, Alan Jackson, George Jones, and Bill.

"I'd like to cash this check," she said to the lady inside the teller's cage. "It's from some politician and I don't trust politicians one bit."

The teller took one look at the check, stamped the back of it, and handed Tammy $150 in cash. "It's OK, honey," she said. "You can trust this politician. He's my husband."

(That lady, by the way, doesn't work in a bank anymore. Today, she has a slightly larger job. She is Shirley Miller, First Lady of the State of Georgia. Her husband's checks are still cashable enough. Only today he signs them, "Governor Zell Miller").

Grand Ole Opry star Billy Walker tells of once being booked, along with the late Carl Belew, into a schoolhouse auditorium in a small town in Illinois for a matinee and evening performance. Following the matinee, the two artists sought out the promoter, as was the custom, and asked to be paid.

When one entertainer wants to wish another entertainer good luck during a performance, he or she will say, "Break a leg."

It's an expression as old as show business itself, although there seems to be no definitive answer as to where or how it originated. I may have once used the term unadvisedly.

Mary Lou Turner had just come aboard as my duet partner and featured female vocalist, and we were booked to play at Jamboree USA in Wheeling, West Virginia, where she had once been a regular cast member. She wanted more than anything to return in style and give a good performance.

As she waited in the wings backstage, I casually said, "Break a leg." Imagine how guilty I felt later when her foot slipped and wedged between the edge of the stage and a wooden railing. She spent the night in the local hospital and left the next day on crutches. The diagnosis: A broken leg!

The promoter said something about having to go somewhere to get the money, and invited Billy and Carl into the school cafeteria to wait until he returned. "You boys help yourselves to all the food you want," the promoter said, pointing to a large refrigerator packed with sandwiches and soft drinks, "and I'll be right back with the money."

The two singers had not eaten and were beginning to get hungry. "I reached in and got a sandwich and something to drink," Billy said, "and all of a sudden this big ole policeman comes bursting into the room and says, 'You're under arrest!'

"'What for?' I asked him. I thought someone was pulling a joke.

"'For coming into this schoolhouse cafeteria and stealing government property,' the officer replied, and he took out his nightstick and began tapping it slowly across his arm. I began to realize it was no joke.

"And would you believe, the policeman took me and Carl downtown to the jail and booked us! They kept us for awhile, then the one who arrested us said if we knew what was good for us we'd go back to the auditorium, work the night show, and get the heck out of town. And the whole time that big dude was talking he kept right on tapping that nightstick across his arm. We knew it was a set-up, but we got the message. We went back, played the show, and left town, just like he said to do.

"And we never did get paid!"

◆

The maddest I ever saw Patsy Cline was about five days into a long Canadian tour for a promoter who had come up with a different excuse every night for not paying me, Cowboy Copas, Roy Drusky, and Patsy.

"The bank closed before I could get there today," he told us the first night, backstage in a small ice hockey arena somewhere in Ontario. "Go ahead and do the show tonight, and I'll pay you for two days tomorrow." We did. But he didn't.

"My car broke down today and by the time I got it repaired and drove to the bank, the bank was closed," was his reason the second night. "But don't worry. I'll pay you for three days tomorrow." Once again we trusted him. Once again we didn't get paid.

And on it went. The singers continuing to sing and the promoter continuing to stall. By the fourth day, however, he was running out of excuses and Patsy Cline was running out of patience.

"Hoss," she said, (Patsy called everybody "hoss" or "chief"), standing not six inches from him and leaning up into his face, "if you don't pay us tomorrow night before the show, there ain't gonna be no show. You understand what I'm telling you? What there is gonna be *is* one helluva ugly *scene*. You got that?" And she punched her index finger not-so-gently into his ribs.

Patsy Cline and Bill

The promoter nodded his understanding and swore again that the money would be there the following night.

The next night we arrived at the venue in Toronto, set up our equipment, and began, as usual, to get dressed for the show. All except Patsy. She stood alone in the corner of the dressing room in her travelling clothes, her hair tightly rolled in curlers and wrapped in a scarf. The rest of us were smiling at the sound of the sell-out crowd making its way into the auditorium. We could smell a good show coming up and our money coming forth. All but Patsy.

"Y'all can get dressed if you want to, hoss," she said to no one in particular, "but if he don't get his ass in here with the money, I'm tellin' you there ain't gonna be no show. Cline is gonna see to that!" And we laughed. All but Patsy.

About five minutes before eight, the promoter came into the dressing room. He never got a chance to say a word.

"You got my money, Chief?" Patsy asked. And she stuck out her palm.

"Well, I....uh, you see, it's ...."

We never found out what Excuse Number Five-In-A-Row was going to be. Patsy took a big, deep breath, let out an oath I'll not repeat here, and ripped past me and Copas and Drusky as if we weren't even standing there. Still dressed in her baggy slacks, wrinkled blouse, and with her hair still in curlers and a scarf, she swept right out to center stage and grabbed the microphone.

The audience had no idea who she was. She certainly didn't look a thing like the pictures they had seen of Patsy Cline. She looked more like she might have been someone hired to clean the auditorium when the show was over. The house lights were still up and late arrivals were still trickling in through the back door.

"I gotta tell you folks somethin'," Patsy snarled into the open microphone, never pausing to tell the crowd who she was or who she represented. The audience stared and began to slowly grow quiet.

"There ain't gonna be no show tonight," she announced. "We been out here workin' our butts off for this jerk promoter (and she told the crowd his name) for four days before gettin' here, and we ain't got paid yet. I told him last night if he didn't pay us tonight there wasn't gonna be no show. Well, he ain't paid us and we ain't gonna sing. So y'all might as well go on home." And she didn't say goodnight, thanks for coming, or kiss my foot. She stormed off the stage as

Roy Drusky and Bill

defiantly as she had stormed on.

Copas, whose daughter, Kathy, was married to Patsy's manager, Randy Hughes, cringed and grabbed her by the arm. "You shouldn't have done that, Patsy," he began in a fatherly tone, but she didn't care to listen. She pulled away from his grasp, stalked to the dressing room, put on her coat, and headed for our rented car.

The crowd was stunned. Some thought it was a joke and stayed in their seats waiting for the performance to begin. Others began trickling backstage seeking clues as to what was going on. I watched as the promoter slid out the back door, into the front seat of his big, black Cadillac and roared off into the night.

"Hey, are we sticking together or what?" Patsy called out from the front seat of the car. "Let's go to the hotel and have a drink!" Cope, Drusky, and I looked at each other and shrugged. What else could we do? We hadn't been paid either, and none of us had signed to come on tour for our health. We didn't necessarily agree with Patsy's tactics, but we knew she was right. We packed up our clothes and our guitars and climbed into the car alongside her.

We left Canada the next day without having ever been paid a dime for our trip. We flew back to Nashville in Roy Drusky's single-engined private plane. Me and Roy and Patsy Cline and Cowboy Copas. We made it home with no trouble, none of us imagining in our wildest dreams that it would only be a few months until two of the four would climb aboard another private plane headed for home and wouldn't be nearly so lucky.

CHAPTER TWELVE

The country music universe in the early sixties was a much smaller and more intimate sphere than it is today. We were more like a large family than a big business. Everybody knew everybody else—artists buddied around with disc jockeys, DJ's hung out with songwriters, and pickers hooked-up with other pickers at any spot in the road wide enough to host a guitar-pull. It was often said that if one of us got cut, the rest of us bled. And that was true—so true, in fact, that very syndrome precipitated one of the saddest and most trying periods of time in country music history.

It was late in the winter of 1962-'63. A country music disc jockey of many years in the Kansas City area, Jack Call, had been killed in an automobile crash. We all knew him as "Cactus Jack," small in stature but a big man in our industry and big in the eyes and ears of his listeners. Most of us had guested on his radio shows when we had been in the Kansas City area. And we all liked him.

True to the concept of one being cut and the others bleeding, a benefit concert had been set up at Memorial Hall in Kansas City, Kansas, to raise money for Jack's surviving wife and children. I hadn't heard about the show until early the preceding week when Billy Walker called me at home to see if I might be able to fly to Kansas City and take part.

"Some of the artists are flying out in a private plane," Billy had said, "and they'll try to make room for you, too, if you can go. If not, several of us are flying commercial. We're going up Sunday morning and coming back Monday. Can you make it?"

I checked my date book and found I was booked on Saturday night somewhere in the northeast. There was no way I could make flight connections to Kansas City that would get me there by show time. I thanked Billy for calling

O ne night early in my career, I came off stage following what I felt had been a very successful performance, and was met by a lady who, I thought, had come to pay me the compliment of all compliments.

"This is the first time I've ever heard you sing," she offered, "and you remind me of Hank Williams."

I was on top of the world, feeling invincible, and I shot back playfully, "But he's dead."

She replied without so much as the trace of a smile, "That's what I mean."

me, and told him I hoped the show would be a big success.

◆

They say you never forget where you are when tragedy strikes. I remember exactly where I was and who I was with the minute I heard President Kennedy had been shot. And the morning the Challenger exploded. And the night war broke out in the Persian Gulf. And I'll never forget the sound of the telephone next to my bed waking me up before daylight on Wednesday morning, March 6, 1963, a week following Billy Walker's call.

"Bill," the tense, out-of-breath voice of a lady rang into my ear, "have you got your radio on?" It took me a minute to recognize Patsy Crutchfield, wife of my songwriting buddy, Jerry Crutchfield.

"No, why?" I mumbled sleepily into the mouthpiece. I rolled over and tried to brush the cobwebs from my brain.

"Go turn on WSM right now," Patsy ordered. "It's awful. Hawkshaw Hawkins was killed last night in a plane crash." I sat straight up in bed. "Oh, Lord," I said, and I instantly thought of Jean Shepard, Hawk's wife, who was due to have a baby almost any day. And for some reason, I pictured in my mind a giant airliner tumbling through a pitch-black, starless sky.

I ran to the living room and turned on the radio. The first voice I heard was that of veteran Opry announcer, T. Tommy Cutrer.

He was trying to read the news, but his voice was breaking and cracking. He kept pausing as if trying to catch his breath. I had never heard him sound like that in all the hundreds of broadcasts I had heard him deliver. Finally he broke down and began to cry.

I don't know if the details were slow in coming or if I was still half asleep and slow in comprehending, but it took a few minutes for it all to sink in. Hawkshaw Hawkins hadn't been the only one killed, and it wasn't an airliner. It was a private plane, returning from Jack Call's benefit show in Kansas City, and it had crashed in bad weather somewhere in west Tennessee. Where was Camden, Tennessee, anyhow? I had never heard of it before.

Roger Miller, they said, had been one of the first people on the scene and he had found some of the bodies. Bodies? Whose bodies? How many bodies? If this is a bad dream, I'd like to wake up now, please.

But I was awake and it wasn't a dream. It was real. Four people were dead: Hawkshaw Hawkins, Cowboy Copas, Patsy Cline, and Randy Hughes. The voice on the radio kept repeating their names over and over again.

I learned later that while I had slept, Grant Turner had been manning the controls at WSM and had spent most of the evening attempting to separate fact from rumor as news of the tragedy began to slowly trickle in.

"For a long time, we didn't give out the names of any artists we thought might have been on the plane," Grant told me not long before he died in 1991. "Until the actual wreckage was spotted, we held out hope that maybe the plane had landed in a field somewhere and everybody was still alive. I've been credited in movies and books as having been the announcer who first broke the news, but all I announced was that a plane carrying some country music stars was missing and feared down. I got off the air at daybreak and was driving home listening in my car when T. Tommy first told who was on board."

Over and over again the news poured out of my radio. By this time every station in town had the story and it was on television as well. And all the announcers sounded so serious, as if all this talk about a plane crash were really true. When was the laughter going to start? Where was the punch line? When was somebody going to step out from behind the curtain and tell us it was all a big joke and the show would start in ten minutes? I waited, but it never came.

◧

Looking back on it now, it's sometimes hard to separate what I actually remember from what I've read and seen and been told over the years. But I do remember a lot. And it still hurts, because so many of my friends were affected. So many lives were turned upside down. And it's so easy to say it should have never happened.

Most country fans know the facts. Patsy and Cope and Hawk and Randy had all worked the Sunday show in Kansas City—a benefit show for which they had

A Country fan once asked the members of Hank Williams' original Drifting Cowboys Band, "Are you really the guys who played behind Hank Williams?"

To which Don Helms, Hank's steel guitar player replied, "We put him where he is today!"

◧

Another fan asked the band the same question: "Are you really the guys who played behind Hank Williams?"

This time, however, he got a straight answer. "We sure are."

"Wow," the fan exclaimed, "he was my favorite. I wish I had lived long enough to see him!"

New York City was virtually virgin territory for country music in the early 1950's when Hank Williams found himself booked for a series of concerts there in the posh Astor Hotel. Few of the Nashville singers and musicians had ever ventured quite so far out of their natural habitat.

On the day of their arrival in the Big Apple, Hank's bass player and on-stage comedian, Cedric Rainwater, swept into the lobby of the Astor with his suitcase in one hand and his cowboy boots in the other. He flung the boots up onto the check-in counter and commanded the clerk, "Hoss, show me to my stall."

Hank witnessed the incident and chastised his employee. "Ced, you are uncouth," he barked.

Whereupon Cedric snapped right back, "Hoss, I'm just as couth as you are—and maybe couther!"

donated their time and their talents free of charge—and had tried to fly back to Nashville on Monday. The weather had been terrible, however, and Randy was advised not to attempt the flight. By Tuesday afternoon conditions had improved only slightly, but entertainers away from home with nowhere to go and nothing to do oft' times become like caged animals in their hotel rooms. The Code of the Hillbillies has always been to get out of town and start heading home once the last show of the tour has been wrapped and put to bed. So against the advice of the weather professionals, Randy fired up the engines and took off for Music City.

The stars flew with no apparent problems to Dyersburg in west Tennessee, where they landed in the early evening to refuel. Some of them telephoned home to let their families know they would be landing in Nashville in a little over an hour. Randy called the small Cornelia Fort airport on the banks of the Cumberland River to tell them he would be bringing the plane there instead of into the larger Metropolitan Nashville Airport. Knowing Cornelia Fort often closed at sundown, he told the attendant on duty to make sure the runway lights at the little airfield were left on.

It was cloudy and misting rain in Dyersburg. Once again Randy was advised to not take off, but he failed to heed the warning. He was not an experienced instrument pilot, and most flight experts seem to think he flew into the clouds, got confused when he couldn't see the ground, and flew the plane full-speed into the side of a hill a few minutes later.

◈

The heart, spirit, and soul of Music City was in shambles. No disaster of this magnitude had ever hit our close-knit musical family. It was something we had always dreaded in the backs of our minds, but something nobody ever talked about. It was almost as if discussing it would be to tempt the fates.

There wasn't a performer among us who didn't travel at least a hundred thousand miles each year, and even though most of those miles were on the ground, many of them were in bad weather. Oft' times we were tired and sleepy. Tires were slick, roads were wet, schedules were demanding. The law of averages was against us and we knew it. But we always figured if we ignored it maybe it would stay away. And except for a few isolated cases, it had. Until this time.

Phillips-Robinson Funeral Home on Gallatin Road in east Nashville suddenly and unwittingly became home to the music business and its people for more days than I care to remember. Flowers poured in from all over the world, so many, in fact, that they spilled out of the parlors, into the hallways, and out onto the back porch of the gray, wooden building. I recall days and nights of visitation, pickers and singers and friends and fans standing shoulder to shoulder, whispering in quiet tones about what a shame it was, passing silently by the closed caskets, staring at the smiling photographs of the

For years a singer and a guitar player named Arthur "Guitar Boogie" Smith virtually owned the entertainment business in and around Charlotte, North Carolina.

He was on radio, he was on television, and Arthur Smith and His Crackerjacks were one of the top concert attractions in all the Carolinas.

Don Helms tells of the time Hank Williams and the Driftin' Cowboys were passing through a small town in that area en route to a personal appearance. They pulled up to a traffic light in their long, black limousine with the upright bass fiddle strapped to the top of the car. An old-timer, obviously a native of the area and an Arthur Smith fan, was crossing the street in front of Hank's car when he realized he was approaching an automobile full of travelling musicians.

"Hey," he called out excitedly, "are you guys Arthur Smith's Crackerjacks?"

"No, we're...." Don began to answer.

"You ain't?" the old fellow interrupted, obviously disappointed, but never giving Don a chance to explain that the car held Hank Williams and His Driftin' Cowboys from the Grand Ole Opry instead.

"Well, if you ain't Arthur Smith's Crackerjacks," he said, "then whose Crackerjacks are you?"

stars—knowing and yet having a difficult time accepting the fact that those marvelous voices would be stilled forever.

They held a memorial service for Patsy (her funeral and burial would be held later in her hometown of Winchester, Virginia), followed later by funerals and burials for Cope and Hawk and Randy. And then came the stunning, almost incomprehensible aftershock that hit toward the end of Patsy's service when Jack

Anglin, of the highly successful Johnny and Jack singing team, rushing from the barber shop to the funeral home, crashed and was killed when his car failed to make a curve on Due West Avenue.

I was seated in the row directly in front of Kitty Wells and Johnny Wright, her husband and the other half of the Johnny and Jack duet, during the memorial service for Patsy. Our eyes had met as we were filing in, and our heads had shaken in unison and disbelief at the grief each of us felt inside. As the service ended, I turned to speak to them only to see Johnny, in tears, being led to the door.

"What's the matter with Johnny?" I heard someone ask.

"Jack was just killed," one of the directors of the funeral home replied solemnly.

No one could believe it. Four of our soul-mates and friends gone in a plane crash, and before we could even say a final goodbye, another one had been killed in an automobile accident. What in the world was going on? More importantly, when and where was it all going to end?

CHAPTER THIRTEEN

Hawkshaw Hawkins was one of the first country music stars I ever met. He, Jean Shepard, Jimmy Dickens, and Del Wood came to Athens, Georgia, for a concert while I was working there as a disc jockey. In an effort to bring my listeners the very latest in country music news, I took the station's cumbersome old Ampex 500 reel-to-reel tape recorder out to the high school gymnasium and into the dressing rooms backstage to interview the stars prior to their going on stage to perform.

I had never interviewed a celebrity before. I was excited and scared to death at the same time. But Hawk, whom I cornered first, couldn't have been nicer or made me feel any more comfortable. He answered all my questions patiently and with humor.

"Hawk, are you married?" I asked.

"Been married all my life, Bill," he replied.

"Tell me about your last record," I prodded.

"I hope I haven't *made* my last record!" he answered.

And on it went for close to a half-hour. I kept asking questions and he kept answering them. My problem was I didn't know when to quit. Finally, Hawk ran out of time and patience. I'll never forget the way he ended the interview:

"Well, Bill, I don't want to take up any more of your time," he said graciously. "I know you've got lots of songs to play and lots of other things to do, so I'll just thank you and get out of your way." That was so much nicer than what he was probably thinking:

"Listen, you dumb kid. If you ask me one more stupid question I'm gonna throw both you and that antique tape machine out of the window!" From that moment on, I liked Hawkshaw Hawkins a lot.

The oldest son of Hawkshaw Hawkins and Jean Shepard, Don Robin, was born on December 7, 1961, the twentieth anniversary of the bombing of Pearl Harbor.

Throughout his childhood, his parents and others told him repeatedly that his birthday was a special day, the day Pearl Harbor was bombed.

As it would have been with most young children, however, the significance of the occasion was totally lost on young Don Robin until he was around ten years old. At that time he came to his mother one day and asked, "Mom, who did you say got bombed on my birthday, Minnie Pearl?"

I actually had quite a few of his records in my collection at home. Early in his career he had recorded for King Records and had cut several cover versions of other artists's biggest hits. In those days, King Records sold in the stores for 59 cents each, while Decca and RCA Victor Records sold for 79 cents. I didn't have much extra money in my jeans back then, so I'd often end up with a song sung by Hawkshaw Hawkins instead of the original by Ernest Tubb or Eddy Arnold.

He had two songs, though, that I never heard anyone else perform, and I cherished both records. One was a post-World War II country-gospel song called "When They Found The Mighty Atomic Power," and the other was a heartfelt narration called "The Life Of Hank Williams." Hawk had been one of the opening acts scheduled to appear with Hank Williams on New Year's Day, 1953, when Hank died en route to the auditorium in Canton, Ohio. He told the story of that day and that show on record. It was powerful and touching.

Not long before the ill-fated trip to Kansas City, Hawk had recorded Justin Tubb's composition, "Lonesome 7-7203," and evidently had a premonition that the record might click for him. He took a promotion copy to Ralph Emery at WSM autographed, "To Ralph—Play the hell out of it—Hawk."

Sadly, he didn't live to hear Ralph and every other DJ in the country play it hundreds upon hundreds of times. It became the biggest record of his entire career.

◆

When I first started hanging around WSM and the Grand Ole Opry, I thought Cowboy Copas was the unfriendliest, most stuck-up person I had ever seen. He would come off stage and I'd be standing by wanting to speak with him and he'd walk by me like I wasn't even there. No one had ever introduced me to him and I wanted to meet him. But he would never give me the opportunity to even say hello.

I liked his music. His "Signed, Sealed, and Delivered" was a classic, and of all the great versions of "Philipino Baby" that were on the market, Copas' version was my favorite. It was probably because where all the other singers sang the line, "I've come back from Caroline," Cope added, "South Caroline." Having been born in the state of South Carolina myself, I took that to be a great tribute to my home state.

When I finally did get to know Copas, however, I found out my impressions of him had been totally wrong. He was a jewel of a human being. Once on a tour of Michigan, the promoter had not provided a band for several of the acts who were working as singles, and Cope stayed out on stage every night after his part of the show was over and picked guitar behind me and all the others. I never forgot his unselfishness and true professionalism.

I felt I really got to know him one weekend when he and Patsy Cline rode with me in my old two-door green Ford from Nashville to a show in Hendersonville, North Carolina. Stringbean was with us in the car, too, along with Darrell McCall, who went along to help drive and sing tenor with me on the show.

We weren't ten miles east of Nashville, Copas in the front seat riding shot-gun, when he turned around toward the three of us crammed into the tiny back seat and began cracking us up with his dead-on impersonations of actor Percy Kilbride as the irrepressible Pa Kettle. Then he started telling road stories, stories about things that had happened to him and his fellow entertainers back in the forties and early fifties. Some of his tales were so outrageous and so funny that Patsy laughed so hard she literally fell off the back seat and into the floorboard of the car. Stringbean, who was sitting in the middle of the back seat with Patsy on his left and me on his right, helped pull Patsy back up onto the seat and turned to me.

Quietly he took a draw on his pipe and nudged me in the ribs. "Billy Boy," he said softly, "everybody in this car is crazy except me and you."

When Jean Shepard was only eighteen years old, recording one of her first sessions in Studio B at Capitol Records in Hollywood, when someone came in and told her that Nat King Cole was recording across the hall in Studio A. Being a gigantic fan of Mr. Cole's, Jean asked her producer if he would take her to Studio A and introduce her to the pop music great.

The producer agreed, but Jean says when she walked in the room she was totally in awe. Not only was Nat King Cole there, "but there was the largest orchestra I had ever seen in my life. There must have been twenty-five people in the string section alone.

"I told Mr. Cole it was an honor to meet him and then I said, 'I've never seen so many fiddle players in my life.'

"He smiled and said, 'Young lady, over in Studio B they are fiddle players. In Studio A, they are violinists.'"

I agreed.

Then he added, "And I'm not too sure about you!"

◇

The one story Copas told that stands out in my mind as truly indicative of the plight of the travelling musician in the early days had to do with him and a singer-comedian from the Wheeling Jamboree named Lazy Jim Day. He and Jim were close friends and at one time toured together almost constantly. Back in those days, the tours were often long, drawn-out affairs that lasted for weeks on end.

"We had been away from home forever," Copas said, "and we didn't have one clean piece of clothing between us. Everything we had was dirty—shirts, socks, underwear, everything. We hadn't been able to stop in any one town long enough to send any clothes to the cleaners. Finally our schedule eased up a bit and we checked into a hotel where we could spend the night and not have to leave until late the following afternoon. First thing we did was ask the maid if the hotel had laundry service.

> **I**n the days when large and lush string sections first began replacing fiddles on country records, an interviewer asked Loretta Lynn to explain the difference between a fiddle and a violin.
>
> "That's easy," she said as only Loretta could. "A fiddle is a fiddle, and a whole bunch of fiddles is a violin."
>
> ◇
>
> An overly-zealous record producer once booked a drummer to play on a Grandpa Jones recording session without having first sought Grandpa's approval.
>
> Grandpa, who has always been an exponent of the pure, traditional mountain sound of music, wasn't particularly excited about having drums on his record.
>
> The producer, sensing he may have done the wrong thing, cautiously asked, "Grandpa, do you want drums on this song?"
>
> Not wanting to offend the drummer, who was already in the studio and listening to the conversation, Grandpa tactfully replied, "Very little—if any!"

"She said no, they didn't. But she had a solution if we needed to get some clothes cleaned. '"Just give me your dirty clothes,' she said, 'and I'll take them home with me when I leave this afternoon. I'll wash them tonight at my house and bring them back when I come in first thing in the morning.' It sounded like a good idea to me and Jim, so we unloaded our suitcases and gave her everything we had except the clothes we would need to wear on the show that night.

"We did the show, and on the way back to the hotel ole Jim got to wanting something to drink real bad. We drove from one end of that little town to the other, but we couldn't spot a beer joint or a liquor store anywhere. When we got to the hotel we asked the bellman where we might find a drink.

"'You boys are in a dry county,' he said. 'Nothing to drink around here.'

"'Isn't there *anywhere* we can get a drink?' Jim asked him.

"'Well, I've been told that there's a bootlegger out in the county several miles from here that'll sell you just about anything you want,' the bellman said. 'You could never find where he lives, though, and it'd cost you a fortune to ride out there in a cab.' We didn't care. By this time we were *both* thirsty. All of a sudden, money and distance didn't matter.

"So we called a cab and off we went. He must have driven us twenty-five miles from town, up and down tiny, winding roads until finally the pavement ran out. But he kept on going. In about a half-hour, the cab driver turned off the gravel road and into the driveway of a house.

"I'll never forget it as long as I live. As the cab swung up in front of the bootlegger's place, the headlights lit up the entire yard. And right there, in front of our eyes, was a clothesline full of clothes blowing in the breeze.

"I thought, 'Boy, that's a shirt just like one I've got.' And ole Jim started to say, 'I've got some overalls just like those,' when it hit us. Those were *our* clothes hanging on that line!

"We laughed 'til we hurt. We decided the maid at the hotel must have been the bootlegger's wife. Or his girlfriend. But by the time we got over the shock of seeing our clothes flapping in the wind in their back yard, we didn't care who was married to whom or who lived where. All we wanted was that drink!"

◆

The first time I met Patsy Cline, I was struck by how much younger she looked in person than I had thought her to be. I later learned she was only twenty-nine when she was killed, the same age at death as Hank Williams.

I had missed her legendary performances on the Arthur Godfrey Talent Scouts show and couldn't recall ever having seen her on any other television shows at that time. I had seen pictures of her, however, and I had seen her album covers. From those I had judged her to be a heavy-set, middle-aged lady. When we met, I found her to be much trimmer and much more youthful than I had imagined. And she was *so* full of life.

At some point, not long after she moved to Nashville, she signed with the Hubert Long Agency for personal appearance bookings. Since I was represented by Hubert as well, Patsy and I began to be booked and to travel on show dates together. It's hard to believe now, with Patsy being a member of the Country Music Hall Of Fame—her name prefaced by "the immortal," but until "I Fall To Pieces" came along, she opened the shows and I closed them.

◆

In his early days as a touring performer, the founder of bluegrass music, the great Bill Monroe, often wandered far off the beaten path to find musicians who could play and sing his highly specialized type of music. It was music rooted in the hearts of people who, like Bill, were from the backwoods areas of Kentucky, Tennessee, and Virginia, and his seeking out players who were virtually born with guitars, banjos, and mandolins in their hands resulted, more than once, in his hiring new band members who had never ventured very far out into the modern-day world.

The story goes that Bill once hired a musician for his band who had never before eaten in a restaurant. On this young man's first day out on the road, the Bluegrass Boys stopped for lunch. The boy was nervous and didn't know exactly what to do, so when the waitress came and began taking everyone's order he decided to listen and order whatever the other band members were having.

The little cafe was featuring a special that day on corned beef and cabbage, and everybody in the group seemed to be setting on that. When it came the new boy's turn, he told the waitress to bring him the corned beef and cabbage, too.

The waitress returned in a few minutes with the steaming hot plates and began setting them down around the table. The boy who had never before eaten in a restaurant took one look at his plate and grabbed the waitress by the arm.

"Hey," he said, "this ain't what I ordered."

"Yessir, it is," the waitress politely affirmed, pointing to the generous helpings on his plate. "It's corned beef and cabbage."

"Oh, yeah?" the young man replied. "Then where's my corn?"

In the summertime, a lot of the Opry acts worked on Sunday afternoons at a small amusement park outside Chattanooga called Lake Winnepesaukah. Patsy and I were booked there together on several occasions.

Allowing for the one-hour time difference between the Central and the Eastern time zones, we would usually leave Nashville early on Sunday mornings, stop along the way for breakfast, and pull into Chattanooga just in time to change clothes and be on stage for our first show at two o'clock.

There was only one slight problem. There were no backstage dressing rooms at Lake Winnie. The entertainers had to change clothes either (a) in the car, or (b) inside the locker room by the swimming pool. My first introduction to the wide range of expletives in Patsy Cline's vocabulary came on the first Sunday afternoon she had to put on her stage clothes standing next to a half-dozen, dripping-wet teeny boppers inside the swimming pool locker room!

I went to Patsy's home on several occasions, once or twice to try and interest her in recording some songs I had written. She seemed to like my writing, but we never connected on anything. I've really wished over the years that we had, because Patsy had that rare ability to extract emotion from a song that oft' times exceeded the emotion the songwriter put into the song in the first place. That, coupled with Owen Bradley's timeless record production techniques, have served to make Patsy's music just as relevant today as it was thirty years ago.

There was no denying her tremendous talent. There was no denying her zest for living either. Late one night in Toronto, she knocked on the door of my hotel room.

"Hoss, have you looked out your window?" she exclaimed, brushing right past me and pulling open my curtains. "What," she asked, "is *that*?"

I rushed over to the window not knowing what to expect, only to find myself looking down upon a cadre of Royal Canadian Mounted Police idling on horseback in the middle of the street. They didn't seem to be embarked on any great mission, but admittedly they were resplendent in their full-dress uniforms: bright red coats, dark trousers, and high, fur-covered hats. Patsy had evidently never seen anyone dressed like that in her life.

"They're RCMP's," I told her matter of factly.

"They are what?" she asked.

"Royal Canadian Mounties," I repeated. "They're policemen."

"They're policemen? Hoss, we ain't got no police back home look like that!"

I laughed.

"I'll tell you one more thing," she said, reaching down and rubbing her right hand across the top of the wedding ring on her left hand. "If ole Cline wasn't a married lady, I'd go down there right now and get me one of those!"

I laughed again. I had learned long before not to be shocked or surprised by anything Patsy Cline said or did. She pushed the curtains back a little farther.

"I believe I'll take me one more look," she said, "then I'm

When country singer Jim Owen was seen on a local television station in Kentucky, he was once approached by a young singing hopeful who wanted to make a guest appearance on Jim's show.

"We're not in production right now," Jim tried to explain.

"But I see you on my TV every week," the young man replied.

"Yes," Jim said patiently, "but those are re-runs."

"Well," the anxious, would-be star countered, "can I be on one of those?"

gonna go call home and talk to ole Charlie Dick on the telephone."

I stood by the window and watched her peer out into the street for another two or three minutes. She sighed, then turned and walked slowly out my door and back down the hall to her room.

I waited until I heard the opening of her door, then the closing, followed by the clicking of her bolt lock. It was only then that I felt secure that the Royal Mounties were safe from Patsy Cline.

More importantly, I knew Patsy was safe from herself.

CHAPTER FOURTEEN

Sadly, the menace of tragedy that has stalked country music for years did not end with the deaths of three of its biggest stars in 1963. As recently as 1991, seven members of a country music entourage, musicians and support personnel working for superstar Reba McEntire, were killed in the crash of a chartered jet in southern California. Later that same year, singer Dottie West died from injuries suffered in an automobile wreck en route to a performance at the Grand Ole Opry.

Dottie West and Bill

Every time catastrophe descends upon our business, the tabloid press starts screaming about the "Star-Crossed Country Music Business." A lot of people seem to be convinced that our industry is cursed by a jinx.

It was less than a month after the 1963 plane crash that a Nashville singer named Texas Ruby, wife of country fiddling great, Curly Fox, and a former member of the Grand Ole Opry, was burned to death when her house trailer caught fire. On July 31, 1964, the man they called "Gentleman" Jim Reeves, one of the smoothest-singing balladeers country music has ever known, was killed when his private plane crashed attempting to land at the Nashville airport during a violent thunderstorm. And on November 11, 1973, in one of the saddest and most senseless of crimes, Dave "Stringbean" Akeman and his wife, Estelle, were brutally murdered inside their rural Nashville home following

String's Saturday night appearance on the Grand Ole Opry.

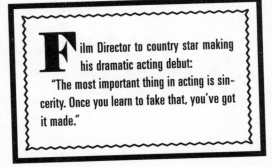

Film Director to country star making his dramatic acting debut:

"The most important thing in acting is sincerity. Once you learn to fake that, you've got it made."

◆

Jim Reeves' death hit me close to home, literally and figuratively. We weren't bosom buddies, but Jim had recorded several of my songs and we had toured quite a bit together. His recordings of two of my compositions, "I Missed Me" and "Losing Your Love," are both considered country classics.

I was at home alone, downstairs in my combination office and songwriting room, the Friday afternoon his plane went down. I didn't know it at the time, of course, but Jim's body and the twisted wreckage of the single-engined Beechcraft lay in a clump of trees no more than a few hundred yards from my window.

My wife had come in around 3:30 or four o'clock that afternoon to tell me she was going to the grocery store to pick up a few things for dinner. I would have probably gone with her except for the fact that I was planning to leave town on a road trip around ten o'clock that night, and I felt a need to stay home and take care of a few last-minute details.

About 4:30, I heard loud thunder begin to roll, and I looked out my window into one of the darkest, most foreboding skies I had ever seen. In a matter of only a few minutes, the winds began to blow furiously, the heavens opened up, and a vicious storm began to unleash its fury. The raindrops were so big and falling with such force that it sounded as if my roof were being pelted with baseballs. I got up out of my chair and walked to the window. The rain was so dense I couldn't even see my daughter's swing set out in the yard, no more than ten feet away.

It was more than an hour before my wife returned from the store, apologizing for being late. "I had to pull over to the side of the road and just sit there," she said. "I've never seen it rain so hard in my life."

I helped her in with the groceries then turned on the news to try and catch the weather forecast. My band and I would be heading north toward Chicago in just a few hours, and I was anxious to know if the storms were moving in that direction.

About five minutes into the newscast, the anchor was handed a bulletin. It said that the station had received unconfirmed reports that a small airplane had disappeared off the radar screen at Nashville's Berry Field only a short time before. There would be further details, he said, as they became available.

"I'm not surprised," my wife said as she slid a tray of biscuits into the oven. "I don't see how anybody could have flown through that storm." I shook my head and didn't think much more about it.

Later that night, however, as I was driving to pick up the band to leave on our road trip, Ralph Emery announced solemnly on his radio show that not only was a small plane believed to be down, but it was suspected that a country music star might have been at the controls. He gave no names, however, as nothing had yet been confirmed.

I quickly began to try and figure out who it might be. My first thought was Roy Drusky since I had flown with him many times. Then I thought of Earl Scruggs. I knew he piloted his own plane. Jim Reeves never crossed my mind. I was not even aware that Jim had his pilot's license.

When I reached Jimmy Gateley's house, where the band had gathered, I headed straight for the telephone. I called Ralph at WSM and asked him who was on the plane.

"Bill, I'm afraid it's Jim," he answered solemnly.

"Jim who?" I asked, still not making the connection.

"Jim Reeves," Ralph said. "He and Dean Manual (his piano player) had been to Arkansas on business. Supposedly, they had made contact with the control tower and were trying to make it in when the storm hit. It doesn't look good." The sad tone of Ralph's voice surprised me. I had been told that he and Jim Reeves were not the closest of friends.

I called home and told my wife what I had learned. She had some news for me as well.

"It must have crashed close to here," she said, "because just about the time you left, helicopters started flying over our house real low. They were shining searchlights all over the place. And I just now looked out the window and a whole lot of people are walking up and down our street with flashlights. Looks like a search party."

I wanted to go back home and join the hunt, but we had to head northward. "I'll call you when we stop for gas," I said. "Keep me posted as best as you can." She assured me she would.

We were a somber group as we loaded our musical instruments and stage clothes into our small fiberglass trailer, locked the rear doors, slid across the red leather seats of the long white

Young Marty Stuart, who played on the Opry with Lester Flatt at the age of thirteen, and is now one of the Opry's newest members:

"I had a school teacher who told me I could make something out of myself if I would get my mind off music and get it on to history. I told her that I was more into making history than learning about it."

Jim Reeves

Cadillac, and rode off into the night.

I thought about Jim, his wife Mary, and how our lives had touched as I drove through the darkness toward Chicago.

I had first met Jim in my disc jockey days when he came to Atlanta for a concert. He had been cordial and had autographed a picture for me to take to the radio station. In those days his band had been known as the Wagon Masters, a fact not many people remember now that that same name is more closely associated with Porter Wagoner. Jim had dressed them in colorful western attire. He had worn tailored western clothes himself and I had been impressed. I have always been partial to stage wear that sets the performers apart from the people in the audience. Later in his career, of course, Jim would come to perform almost exclusively in dinner jackets and far more conservative costumes.

When I first moved to Nashville, I worked a few isolated show dates with Jim, including a small county fair one Saturday night in Benton, Kentucky. I rode to Benton with Jim and his band in a station wagon, and I remember how Jim got to craving an ice cream cone along the way. He had everybody in the group searching both sides of the highway trying to spot a Dairy Dip.

Later we worked a long tour together where Jim and the promoter got into a big argument over whether or not Jim's band (by this time known as the Blue Boys) was to provide the music for me and several other singers on the show who did not, at that time, have our own bands. The promoter had been under the impression that Jim would allow his band to work with us. Jim said, no, the band was for his use only.

Since there was no other band on the tour, Jim's refusal to let his band work with anyone but him placed a tremendous burden on the rest of the cast. But, as we often did back in those days, everybody pitched in and helped work it out.

Don Helms was playing steel with the Wilburn Brothers and they agreed to open the shows. When their part was over Don would stay on stage and play behind the other acts. So would Lester Wilburn, the bass player. Doyle and Teddy Wilburn, stars themselves, alternated nights playing rhythm guitar. This was the tour where Cowboy Copas, who went on stage after the Wilburns, hung around and picked lead guitar on his flat-top Martin for anyone who wanted. And even June Webb, the female singer on the tour, helped out with background harmonies when necessary. It wasn't a very fancy band or a very good band, but it worked. The fans, who didn't know of all the backstage hassles, sensed something very special was taking place on stage and they loved it.

At the time, I didn't comprehend Jim Reeves' refusing to let his band work with us. Later, when I formed my own band, I came to a better understanding of the situation. They were his band, he had hired them and trained them, and he paid them to play his music and help him look good on stage. To allow them to work haphazardly with little or no rehearsal behind the other acts would diminish their uniqueness and their value to him. I understand that now. But at the time I can't say that I did. Likewise, I have never refused to let my band work behind other singers as long as my group wants to do it, as long as they have sufficient rehearsal time, and as long as they are compensated for their efforts.

When singer-songwriter Hoyt Axton finally got his first No. 1 record, he naturally expected to receive several thousand dollars in royalties. After all, the record not only reached No. 1, but it stayed at the top of the charts for three weeks. He was shocked when the check came from his publisher and it totaled only $800.

"He told me I had signed the wrong paper or something," Hoyt sheepishly says today. "I started to press charges against him, but somehow I couldn't bring myself to sue over a song called, "I Don't Give A Damn About A Greenback Dollar."

◆

I thought for awhile that I was going to be the writer of Jim Reeves' follow-up record to his million-selling crossover smash, "He'll Have To Go." He cut my song, "I Missed Me," on one of his next sessions, but then decided to hold it and release another song first. The second song didn't come close to equalling the success of "He'll Have To Go," particularly in the pop field, and by the time my song came out next, some of the Jim Reeves' momentum had begun to wane.

One of the strong selling points of "He'll Have To Go" had been Jim's uncanny ability to caress the low notes in the third line of the song:

"Tell the man to turn the jukebox way down low..."

When Jim sang the word "low," he really reached down deep on the musical scale, but he always hit the note right on the button. Later, I came to understand how he did it.

I was at his house one afternoon when a company of sound technicians had come to install a package of new recording equipment in his basement. Jim was in the process of having a small studio built so that he could record demonstration tapes of new songs without ever having to leave home. Many country artists, particularly those who write songs or are in the music publishing business, have similar set-ups.

The technicians were fine-tuning the new equipment and asked if I'd mind stepping over to where they were working and putting on a pair of earphones. I did, and they connected me to a bunch of wires and meters.

"Tell us when you can hear the tones," they instructed, and in a minute I began to hear piercing sounds, like feedback, in each ear. I signaled that everything was coming in loud and clear. They were making notes on a sheet of paper.

"Now tell us when you can't hear the tones anymore," they said, and the pitch of the tones began to rise. Higher and higher they went. I heard the next tone, then the next, and the next, and the next. Finally the tones became so shrill and so high-pitched that I couldn't hear them anymore. I signaled to the technicians that I had lost the sound completely.

"Great, now let's do the same thing with the low tones," they said. They repeated the whole process in reverse, with the tones gradually becoming lower and lower on the musical scale. The low tones disappeared faster in my ears, though, than had the high tones. I let them know when I couldn't hear them anymore.

"OK, Jim, now you step over here and let's try you," they said to Jim Reeves. He did as he was told and the technicians went through the whole process again. But there were two notable differences: Jim lost the high tones several decibels before I had lost them. And he could hear the low notes a good four to six d.b. lower than I could.

"I can't believe you can't hear that," he said to me as one of the low tones rumbled in his ears. "I can hear it perfectly." I put the headphones back on and I couldn't hear a thing. I knew the tone was being played, however, because I could see it registering on the meter. Then the technicians switched to the high tones. The same thing happened in reverse. I could hear tones much higher than Jim could.

"I guess that's why you're the great ballad singer and I sing 'Po' Folks' and do recitations," I said. He smiled and seemed to be pleased.

◆

We reached Chicago around mid-morning on Saturday and there was still no word from Nashville on the fate of the missing plane. It had become common knowledge that Jim Reeves

> **L**egendary record producer Owen Bradley on why he liked to vary the type of songs his artists recorded, even when they were having hits with one particular kind:
>
> "It's great to be in a groove, but if you stay in a groove too long it becomes a rut."

was the pilot, however, and my wife said it seemed the whole town was involved in the search.

"Helicopters have been flying so close to our sun deck I could almost reach out and touch them" she said when I called. "They never stopped all night. People are walking all over our yard, up through the woods in back, everywhere in this area. They think he crashed somewhere between here and Brentwood."

I hung up and thought of my disc jockey friend of many years, Uncle Len Ellis, who broadcast country music on a station just south of Chicago. I decided to give him a call to see if perhaps he had received any information on the crash from off the station's news wire.

"No, I haven't even heard about it," Len said when he came on the phone. "That's terrible. I've booked Jim on a lot of shows, you know." I knew he had. Len Ellis had booked us all.

He then asked if I would mind his patching my phone call into his control board so I could talk to his listeners. I agreed, and proceeded to tell him and his listeners what little I knew.

◆

They found Jim Reeves' plane late Sunday afternoon resting in a dense clump of trees just over the hill from my house. There were no survivors.

More talk of a jinx or a hex on the entertainment business surfaced almost immediately, with reminders of previous tragedies, ranging from the 1959 plane crash that killed Buddy Holly to the Patsy Cline crash the previous year screaming from off the front pages.

To those of us closer to the scene, it was a quieter, more reflective time. Another friend of ours was gone. Another magnificent voice had been stilled. And while the presses roared and people rushed to read the headlines, the singers and songwriters and musicians who built this marvelous city of music paused and wept again.

Connie Smith and Bill

A lady stopped me outside my dressing room at the Grand Ole Opry. She said, "I want to thank you."

I asked, "For what?"

And she replied, "For inventing Connie Smith."

CHAPTER FIFTEEN

I t has been common knowledge among the artists in country music for quite some time that Porter Wagoner doesn't like to fly on airplanes. For years, if he couldn't make it to a show date by riding on his tour bus, he wouldn't go at all. I only recently found out why.

"In the late fifties," Porter told me one night at the Opry, "I had worked a date in San Francisco and Don Warden, my manager, had booked us on an early morning flight to our next show. I think it was in Texas. Anyhow, we were scheduled to leave around seven o'clock the following morning.

"When we got back to our hotel after the show, though, we were both so tired that I asked Don to check and see if we could take a later flight. He called and found one that left around eleven o'clock and would still get us where we needed to go on time. We cancelled the early flight, booked the later one, and slept in.

"The next morning when we got to the airport, we heard there had been a crash. Two planes had collided over the Grand Canyon. One of them was United Flight #711, the flight we had originally been booked on.

"I've had a hard time getting back on airplanes ever since. In fact, I've still got my unused ticket at home. Sometimes I'll take it out and look at it. It's easy then to climb right back on my bus."

◆

Over the years, Little Jimmy Dickens has preferred to travel and transport his band to and from their personal appearance dates in a van as opposed to a plane or a larger, more luxurious customized bus.

Once, prior to leaving for a tour in Texas, he hired some new band members who assumed they would be travelling by bus. When they realized they would be riding in a van, however, they began complaining in voices loud enough for Jimmy to hear, "Everybody we know has a bus." Day after day as the tour unfolded they griped to anyone who would listen, repeating over and over, "Everybody we know has a bus."

Finally, when the tour ended and the van was headed for home, an irritated Little Jim got his revenge.

"I waited until everybody was asleep," he says, "and went to the Greyhound bus station. I bought them tickets to Nashville. Then I set their instruments out on the street and woke them up.

"I said, 'OK, boys, you can ride the bus now.'"

◆

One night at the old Ryman Auditorium, Grandpa Jones was late arriving for his appearance on the Friday night Grand Ole Opry. When he finally came into the dressing room, we all wanted to know why he was late.

"I've lost one of my cows," he explained, "and I've been out all day a-lookin' for her. I can't find her anywhere."

In the true spirit of the Opry, several of the stars who lived near Grandpa volunteered to come out to his farm early the next morning and help him continue his search. Saturday night Grandpa walked into the Opry right on schedule.

"Did you find your cow, Paw?" I asked him.

"I found 'er," Grandpa answered.

"Where was she?" I asked.

"In the dad-blamed freezer," he replied sheepishly. "We'd be a-eatin' on 'er fer two weeks!"

◆

When the Opry first moved from the Ryman to its new home at Opryland USA, the Opry stars were not assigned parking places in the backstage parking areas as they are today. Grandpa probably had a lot to do with our receiving our special numbered spaces.

He arrived at the Opry one night, drove in through the security gate, and couldn't find a place to park his car. Angry and frustrated, he drove right back out the gate and returned to his home at Ridgetop, north of Nashville.

When it came time for Grandpa's appearance on the stage he was nowhere to be found. Anxiously, one of the Opry officials began trying to locate him and, fearing he might be ill, called his home. He was shocked and quite worried when Grandpa himself answered the telephone.

"Paw, are you all right?" he asked.

"I'm fine," Grandpa replied.

"Well, why aren't you at the Opry?"

Grandpa was ready with his answer: "If I ain't good enough to park," he said, "I ain't good enough to pick."

We all had assigned parking places the next week.

Bill and Grandpa Jones

◆

Grandpa Jones stories could fill volumes much thicker than this one.

One of my favorites took place when Grandpa and the late Opry star, Stoney Cooper, were each hospitalized at the same time. Grandpa had surgery for gallstones. Stoney had suffered a serious heart attack.

Stoney's wife and singing partner of many years, Wilma Lee Cooper, had left Stoney's bedside and gone to Grandpa's room for a visit. In the course of conversation, she asked Grandpa how many get-well cards he had received from his fans.

"Wail, I've gotten a few," Grandpa answered slowly in his patented nasal tones, "maybe twenty or twenty-five."

"Stoney's received *hundreds* of cards from our fans," Wilma Lee said. "Aren't they wonderful? They've sent him just hundreds and hundreds of cards."

"Wail, Wilmer," Grandpa replied, his mind ever in the show business vernacular, "I guess gallstones just don't draw as good as heart attacks!"

◆

Grandpa said it once rained so much at his house that he didn't know whether to "pave the drive or stock it with fish!"

◆

It is often several degrees cooler in Ridgetop, where Grandpa lives, than it is in Nashville.

One winter's day when it was snowing heavily throughout middle Tennessee, a friend called Grandpa to find out how much snow was on the ground in Ridgetop.

Grandpa said, "Oh, it's about axle deep . . ."

"I'm surprised," his friend interrupted. "That's about what it is here."

". . . to a ferris wheel," Grandpa finished.

◈

Grandpa once travelled to Alabama as a celebrity guest at George "Goober" Lindsay's annual charity golf tournament. For his efforts in entertaining the golfers and their guests at a banquet during the tournament, Grandpa was presented with a pair of shiny, new golf shoes. Somebody asked him how he liked them.

"They'll be all right," Grandpa answered, "soon as I git the tacks out!"

◈

And then there was the time Grandpa was booked for a concert near Ft. Wayne, Indiana, and ended up in Terre Haute, Indiana, some two hundred miles to the south, by mistake.

"I knew the town had two words in it," he said apologetically. "It's a wonder I didn't go to Buenos Aires!"

Opry star Justin Tubb on growing up as the son of a legend:

"When I was a young boy, people would say to me, 'I guess Ernest Tubb is your hero.'

"I would say, 'No, Hank Williams is my hero. Ernest Tubb is the man I see around the house everyday in his underwear.'"

CHAPTER SIXTEEN

I don't want to turn what is intended to be a lighthearted look at the early days of the country music business into a morbid tale of tragedy and heartbreak, but neither do I want to pass over the opportunity to share this next story. To me, this man and one plaintive comment he made to a fellow entertainer sum up so much of what the early era of country music was all about. And in order for this story to be fully effective, I need to sketch in just a bit of unhappy background.

Dave Akeman, known to Grand Ole Opry and "Hee-Haw" fans simply as "Stringbean," was one of the most remarkable human beings it has ever been my privilege to know. I've already related how unflappable he could be in the face of adversity, but I only scratched the surface.

String, as we all called him, once embarked on a fishing trip with Tompall Glaser, of the singing Glaser Brothers, a trip they had been planning for weeks. The morning of their long-awaited venture they met at the boat dock and began to load the small fishing boat with all their gear. They brought aboard tackle and rods and reels and bait and plenty of sandwiches and drinks for the anticipated all-day affair. Once everything was in place, String climbed to his seat, put on his life jacket (he never learned to swim), lit his pipe, and waited for Tompall to shove the boat away from the dock and climb aboard.

Just as Tompall gave a push and went to jump in the boat, however, his foot slipped and Tompall, Stringbean, fishing gear, food, bait, and all were upended and sent plunging into the chilly, waist-deep water.

Stringbean never said a word. While Tompall scurried to upright the overturned boat and to apologize profusely for his blunder, String simply stood there in his bright orange life vest and went about the business of picking up his tack-

Dave Akeman, aka Stringbean

le box, gathering together his belongings, and continuing to puff on his pipe.

The outing they had planned for so long was totally wiped out. There was no way they could do anything but retrieve as many of their personal belongings as possible and make their way slowly back to land. As Tompall apologized for the umpteenth time, String simply took a draw on his pipe, looked at Tompall and said, "Chief, we'll have to go again sometime."

◆

Those of us who knew Stringbean knew that he wasn't a big fan of banks. I rarely knew him not to have a big roll of bills stuffed into the top zipper pocket of his overalls.

Evidently, the fact that String carried large amounts of cash on his person was also not lost on some of his neighbors in the small rural community where he lived. His disdain for putting his cash into banks probably ended up costing him his life.

Most people remember the story: String had performed on the Opry and returned home late on Saturday night. When he and his wife, Estelle, entered their house, they were surprised by intruders. In the ensuing scuffle, the prowlers—two cousins who lived nearby—robbed then shot and killed both Stringbean and his wife.

It was a brutal crime, one that so incensed the Nashville community that public pressure for the authorities to locate and prosecute the killers never let up until the attackers were arrested, convicted, and behind bars. There was never a more beloved figure in all of country music than Stringbean.

◆

The essence of the man—what his values were, where his priorities lay—was revealed in simple eloquence on a night when he was talking with a fellow Opry performer in the alley behind the Ryman Auditorium.

The management of the Opry had recently informed the members of the cast of a new rule: Beginning immediately, all Opry performers would be required to appear on the Opry a minimum of twenty-six weeks every year. Failure to comply would result in the artist's being suspended from the show.

It was a tough rule, but one the Opry figured at the time was a necessity. Fans had begun complaining to management that they were driving hundreds of miles to Nashville to see the Opry, only to arrive and find many of their favorite performers out of town on tour. By passing the twenty-six-week rule, Opry officials felt they could better control their roster and assure the fans of a representative show each weekend.

From the artists' point of view, however, appearing twenty-six times a year on the Opry would be difficult. Most Opry stars could make considerably larger sums of money on tour than they could make staying home and working the Opry for union scale wages. As you might imagine, news of the impending twenty-six-week rule triggered much commotion within the Opry family.

Backstage in the dressing room, in the corridors, across the alley at Tootsie's famed Orchid Lounge, the new rule was all everybody wanted to talk about.

"You gonna make your twenty-six?" one artist would ask another.

"I don't know. How about you?"

"I don't know either. I want to be on the Opry, but I've gotta eat, too."

"Yeah, me too. What's so-and-so gonna do?"

"I don't know."

And on it went.

◆

It was in the midst of this melee that Porter Wagoner happened to be walking down the back steps of the Ryman one Saturday night and spotted Stringbean in the alleyway behind the building climbing out the passenger side of his brand-new Cadillac sedan. String, even with all the miles he had travelled in

Jeannie Seely and Bill

Jeannie Seely, who won a Grammy Award in the sixties for her torchy recording of "Don't Touch Me," has a laid-back approach to living that often belies her quick wit and razor-sharp mind:

"I've spent most of my life just letting the chips fall," the blonde Opry star says, "and now all of a sudden I realize I'm up to my butt in sawdust!"

Once when I was fighting a bout with laryngitis I made the mistake of whispering to Jeannie, "I've lost my voice."

To which she replied, "Really? How can you tell?"

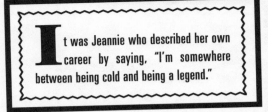

It was Jeannie who described her own career by saying, "I'm somewhere between being cold and being a legend."

his career, had never learned to drive. Estelle drove him everywhere he went.

Porter, who was one of String's best buddies, walked around and began to admire the new car. String usually bought a new Cadillac every year, and the word around the Opry was that he always paid cash.

"Mighty sharp car, hoss," Porter offered, looking admiringly at the new vehicle.

"Thank you, my boy," String replied and Estelle smiled. And then almost immediately talk turned to the new Opry rule.

"You gonna make your twenty-six weeks?" Porter asked.

String never hesitated. It was not, in his mind, a question to ponder. He simply took a deep draw on his pipe and ran his hand across the top of the shiny new luxury sedan. With his fingers still stroking the vinyl roof, he looked Porter straight in the eye.

"My boy," he answered slowly and profoundly, "I came here awalkin'!"

◆

Stringbean, en route to a concert performance, to the driver of an automobile carrying him faster than he cared to travel:

"Slow down, my boy, slow down. I'd rather 'em say 'String was late' than 'the late String!'"

◆

String was always in demand as a performer on the big package shows. He was colorful, musical, comedic, and usually worked alone, saving the promoter precious dollars. Once, on the opening night of a long tour, String looked over the lineup of acts and saw that the show was made up of one major star after another. He thought about it a minute and said, "I'm the only act on this show I never heard of!"

CHAPTER SEVENTEEN

There wouldn't be any country music stars if there were no country music fans. How's that for a brilliant statement?

It's basic, but it's true. Stars need fans to buy their records, attend their concerts, and to support their careers in general. You're probably a fan of something connected with country music or chances are you wouldn't be reading this book. Suffice it to say, none of us in this business could survive without fans.

At the same time, the word "fan" is probably the most misunderstood and misused word in the entire show business vocabulary. Webster's Dictionary defines "fan" as "short for fanatic. An ardent devotee." It goes on to describe a fanatic as "one having excessive zeal for and irrational attachment to a cause or position."

I'm not sure about the "irrational" part, but the rest sounds easy enough to me. And yet I couldn't begin to count all the people who have come up to me over the years and said, "Bill, you're my biggest fan."

It comes out exactly the opposite of what's intended. I know what they mean, though, and most of the time I don't even bother to correct them. I just smile and say, "Why, I've been a fan of yours all my life." They usually reply, "You sure have," and they go away happy. It's backwards, but I guess it works.

The relationship between country music stars and country music fans is unlike anything else in the entire world of entertainment. And it's been that way for as long as anyone seems to remember.

For some reason, the barrier that separates star from fan and fan from star in most other forms of show business exists to a much lesser degree in country music. A smart psychologist could probably write a book thicker than this one on the why's and wherefore's of this particular phenomenon, but my simplified layman's opinion is this:

Most country stars—at least the ones from my generation—have traditionally come from humble backgrounds. They weren't brought up feeling or thinking that they were any better than anyone else. Likewise, en route to whatever stardom they might have achieved, most of them saw to it that their songs remained basic person-to-person music, songs that communicated strong feelings between individuals. Country music is music sung from one heart to another, and it would be impossible to establish the rapport necessary to communicate heartfelt emotions in song if the singer felt he were up on one level and his listener down on another.

Fans, in turn, have told me that they feel many country songs were "written just for me," and while they often put country singers on a pedestal, they don't hold them in awe. They don't feel we're so unlike them that we're unapproachable. It's a unique two-way street that creates a special bonding between country singer and country fan. It's a relationship the rock 'n' roll singers, movie and television stars might envy but could probably never fully comprehend.

"Have you ever had a fan tell you they named one of their children after you?" the legendary Ernest Tubb asked me one hot Sunday afternoon as the two of us rode through west Texas in the front of his tour bus. E.T., as we all called him, had as many or more fans than anyone who ever hit an E-chord on a flat-top guitar, and he treated them with a kindness and a patience that could have qualified him for sainthood.

"Once," I said, recalling a tiny baby with a head full of curly locks that a lady introduced to me as "little Bill" at a concert years before. "I'll bet you've had dozens, though, haven't you?"

"Quite a few," the Texas Troubadour replied. "Did I ever tell you about Ernest Tubb Johnson?" I caught the glimpse

Ernest Tubb and Bill

I toured a lot with the comedy team of Homer & Jethro back in the mid-to-late sixties, and I would always go out of my way to try and check into the hotel or motel at the same time those two zanies would be checking in. It was always good for a laugh.

Homer especially delighted in waiting until an attractive young lady was on duty at the reception desk before he filled out his registration card. Without cracking a smile or saying a word, he would sign his name, his street address, his town and zip code, and then where the card said "Firm," meaning the name of the company where the guest was employed, Homer would invariably write, "Yes."

He'd get everything from laughs to blushes, from astonished looks to come-on's. But he never got ignored.

◈

There's nothing that can grate on an entertainer's nerves any more than having travelled all night to reach the next town on the tour and, for some reason, not be able to check in immediately to a hotel or motel room when he arrives.

We once reached Calgary, Alberta, Canada, after an all-night ride from Montana, and none of the weary souls in our crowded car could remember the name of the Stampeder Motel where we were supposed to stay. With Calgary being the home of the famed Calgary Stampede, I don't know why we couldn't remember the Stampeder Motel, but we couldn't.

"I know it starts with an S," Oscar Sullivan of the Lonzo & Oscar comedy team said drowsily. But he couldn't come up with the name.

Eighteen-year-old Margie Bowes, a naive little country girl from North Carolina who had just won the national Pet Milk Talent Search competition and had never been so far away from home in her life, spoke up innocently from the back seat:

"I don't remember what it starts with, but it has a 'peder' in it!"

Needless to say, our mood lightened considerably.

of a twinkle slowly easing into the corner of his well-travelled eye.

"Ernest Tubb Johnson?" I smiled. "No, I never heard of him."

"It's been quite a few years ago now," Ernest began, "but I'll remember that day and that lady as long as I live. She was the most devoted Ernest Tubb fan in the world, I guess, but she was one of those people who just didn't know when to quit. You know what I mean? It didn't matter how nice I was to her it was never enough."

I nodded. I had run across a few folks in my time who had fit that description pretty well.

"Well, we were working at an outdoor park up east somewhere, and the minute I got off the bus here she came. She had this little baby boy in diapers draped across her arm, and she ran up to me yelling at the top of her voice, 'Ernest, you've got to see my baby. You've got to see my baby. I named him after you. His name is Ernest Tubb Johnson.'

"I stopped and smiled and said, 'Well, honey, that's awful nice,' and I patted the little boy on the head.

"I started to walk away and head for the stage, but she jumped right in front of me. 'Wait, here, you've gotta hold him. I've got to take a picture of Ernest Tubb holding Ernest Tubb Johnson.' And she shoved that little baby right into my arms.

"I stood there and held him and grinned for the camera, and I'll swear she took a whole roll of pictures. When she was through, I handed the baby back to her and started for the stage again. She wanted me to autograph something for her, but I told her I'd have to sign it later. I was about to be late for the show.

"Just as soon as the show was over and I started back for the bus, though, here she came again. She wanted me to sign the boy's baby book. Then his little shoe. And then she wanted to take some more pictures. All day long she kept this up. Once she even asked if I would autograph his diaper. I mean, I couldn't get any rest or visit with any of the other fans for this lady always wanting me to do something for little Ernest Tubb Johnson.

"Finally, we did our second show of the day, and I came off stage all hot and tired and sweaty. I had just about exhausted my patience trying to be nice to this lady, but sure enough, here she came again. 'Ernest, I need one more picture of you and little Ernest Tubb Johnson!' she yelled. I had been as nice to her as I knew how, but I really didn't want to take any more pictures right then. I just wanted to get to the bus and dry off and catch my breath for a minute. So I said to her, 'Honey, not right now,' and I turned to walk away.

"Well, sir, she went crazy. She started screaming at me and yelling at me as to how she had named her baby after me and how I was the most inconsiderate, ungrateful person she had ever known. How dare I treat her like this? Then, just as a I started up the steps of the bus, she called out, 'Well! If I had known you were going to be this way, I would have named him Cowboy Copas!'"

Ernest roared with laughter

The week Garth Brooks sold out three consecutive concerts at Texas Stadium, I received the following letter from a man in Arizona:

"Dear Bill:
I can't see what's so hot about Garth Brooks. How can he even call himself country? He's never been in jail and he's only had one wife!"

as he recounted the story, and I was laughing so hard by this time that I had to grab the edge of the dinette table to keep from falling out into the aisleway of the bus. I could just picture a sweet, innocent little baby boy being saddled with the name "Cowboy Copas Johnson." I thought it was the funniest sounding name I had ever heard. It turned out, though, that E.T. hadn't even gotten to the punch line.

"You know what I told her?" he asked.

I could hardly speak. "What?" I finally managed to ask.

"I shouldn't have done it, I guess, but it had been a long day and that lady had just about worn me out. I turned back to her after she said what she did about Cowboy Copas and I said, 'Lady, right now I don't give a damn if you call the kid Grandpa Jones!'"

◆

No fans get *physically* closer to their heroes than do the fans of country music. Not only do the stars not fight it, they encourage it. Every June, the country music industry invites upwards of 25,000 fans to come to Nashville and take part in a phenomenon known as Fan Fair. The stars play host to the fans for an entire week, and there's nothing like it anywhere else in the world. The record companies stage free concerts, the stars sign autographs, pose for photographs, and even schedule breakfasts, lunches, dinners, and parties with their fans. And the fans walk right up to the stars in the Fan Fair exhibit booths and talk to them like old friends.

"You sure have aged since the last time I saw you," a middle-aged lady informed me at a recent Fan Fair.

"Really?" I smiled, knowing better than to be surprised by anything I might hear from someone who had been standing for hours in a hot, barely-moving autograph line. "When was the last time you saw me?"

"Twenty-five years ago," she replied.

◆

Another lady got my autograph, turned to her husband and, pointing back at me, said to him, "You better hope *you* look that good when *you* get that old!"

◆

Yet another stood in line at my fan club booth for more than an hour to purchase a color, 8 x 10 photograph of me. Then when she reached the spot where I was standing signing autographs, she turned to me with the picture in her hand and a puzzled look on her face. "OK," she said, "now who signs this?"

◈

Reminds me of the time a lady asked the late Tex Ritter for his autograph.

"Why, certainly, my dear," Tex said, taking pen and paper in hand and writing out "Tex Ritter" for her.

When he had finished, he handed the paper back to the lady who looked at it, looked back at Tex, and said, "Oh, I thought you were Gene Autry!"

Whereupon the usually mind-mannered Tex lost control. He grabbed the paper back from the lady, tore his autograph into tiny pieces and threw it on the floor. "Dammitohell, lady," he said, "if you don't know who you're askin', don't ask."

◈

A fan told one of my band members that he had once met singer O.B. McClinton.

"*Before* he died!" the fan exclaimed.

◈

A lady once stopped me at a television studio and asked if I would autograph a piece of paper for her brother who was in the hospital. I said, sure, I'd be glad to. I always try to personalize autographs when I can, so I asked his name, took the paper and wrote: "To Larry—Get well soon—Bill Anderson," and handed it back to the lady.

She took one look at it and wadded the paper up and threw it violently back in my face. "How dare you?" she screamed.

I had no idea what I had done wrong.

"He's not gonna get well," she screamed. "He's going to die. How dare you give him false hope?"

I apologized and told the lady as calmly as I could that I was sorry, I had no way of knowing. I was only trying to cheer him up, but she continued to fume. All I could think of was the old country song, "Sometimes You Just Can't Win."

◈

Porter Wagoner and Dolly Parton could have broken into a chorus of that same tune one night as they were leaving the Ryman Auditorium following an appearance on the Grand Ole Opry. They were at the height of their popularity together, and their bus was waiting in the parking lot to rush them to a sold-out Sunday afternoon performance in eastern Pennsylvania.

"There was a mob of people outside just like there always was at the Ryman," Porter recalls, "and when Dolly and I came out they swarmed all over us asking for autographs. I stood there and as nice and as patiently as I knew how I told them that we wouldn't be able to sign any autographs because we had a one o'clock matinee in Pennsylvania. We *had* to get on the road, and I asked them to please understand.

"Everybody was real nice except this one lady. She kept yellin', 'Come on, Porter. Just sign one. Please, just sign mine.' I told her, 'Darlin', if we sign one we'll have to sign 'em all and we just don't have time. We can't be late for our show.' I was as nice to her as I knew how to be.

"Well, sir, we started making our way through the crowd and up to the steps of our bus and that lady kept after us every step of the way. She screamed and hollered and begged us to sign just one autograph. She said we were her favorite singers of all time. But just as we got to the bus and were about to ride away without having signed anything for her, she changed her tune. 'Well, since you're acting like that,' she yelled, 'I'm glad I voted for Conway Twitty and Loretta Lynn for Duet of the Year!'"

◆

I have always had a natural affinity for children, and over the years I have enjoyed getting children involved in my concerts.

When time allows, I ask if there are any kids in the audience between the ages of, say, seven and nine who think they might want to be singers when they grow up. Invariably several hands will pop up into the air. I survey the scene as quickly as I can, then select one little boy and one little girl to come on stage. I tell them I'll teach them the words if they'll help me sing a song called "The Unicorn." As you might suspect, I have had some interesting experiences.

One little boy got so nervous he wet the stage. A little girl, after she had finished singing the song, reached up and slapped my face. Another boy said he wasn't leaving the stage until I paid him $500 for singing.

When the kids first arrive on stage, I try to engage them in a short conversation in an effort to get them to relax. This also enables me to see just how talkative and uninhibited they might be. If they speak right up, I will sometimes egg them on.

"What's the one thing your mother would not want you to say up here?" I asked one bright-eyed little girl.

"She wouldn't want me to tell you about my Uncle Charlie," the girl answered. "You see, he's not really my Uncle Charlie!"

I quickly changed the subject.

"Where'd you get that red hair?" I asked a carrot-topped little boy in Iowa.

He glared at me without so much as a hint of a smile. "It came with my head!" he answered defiantly.

But the one I'll never forget was the shiny-faced little blonde-haired girl in

South Carolina who couldn't have been more than six years old. She came on stage and immediately began telling me about her boyfriend.

"You have a boyfriend?" I asked.

"I sure do," she replied with a big grin.

"What's his name?"

"Tommy."

"Is Tommy here at the show with you?" I prodded.

"No, he's in Florida."

I couldn't help myself. She was so cute and so talkative. I decided to see just how far she might go.

"Well, let me ask you a question," I teased. "What would you do if you found out that while you were here at my show, Tommy was down in Florida with another girl?"

She never batted an eye. She put her little hand on her hip, looked up at me with a wisdom far beyond her years, and said defiantly, "I'd beat his butt!"

◆

"You're a mighty pretty young lady," I said to another tiny, blonde-haired girl who had stood in line for quite some time waiting for my autograph. She was with her mother at a sponsored personal appearance where I was meeting fans and handing out free pictures. I judged her to be seven or eight years old.

"Are you going to be a singer when you grow up?" I asked.

"No," she replied with a smile.

"What are you going to be?" I prodded as I wrote my name on a picture for her.

"A news anchor on TV," she replied confidently.

"Wow, that's great!" I said, handing her the autographed picture. "I wish you good luck."

"Thanks," she said, and she turned to leave. She took only a couple of steps, however, then turned her head and looked back at me over her shoulder.

"By the way," she called out, "I've never heard of you."

◆

The waitress had passed by our table three or four times during the course of the meal and finally she stopped.

"Excuse me, sir" she said, looking directly at me, "but I couldn't help overhearing you talk. You sound exactly like that man who does those commercials on TV."

"Oh, really?" I asked, assuming she had heard me advertise PoFolks Restaurants, Stanback Headache Powders or perhaps Homelite Chain Saws. "What commercials?"

"For Jimmy Dean Sausage," she replied.

The loyalty of country music fans is legendary. Grand Ole Opry singer and funny-man Johnny Russell says there sometimes seems to be no length to which a true country music fan wouldn't go to be in the presence of his or her favorite star.

He backs that up by telling the story of once being on the Opry stage and looking out into the front row of the audience and seeing the strangest of all sights—an empty seat.

The announcer at the side of the stage was reading a commercial, so Johnny leaned down and asked the lady sitting next to the empty seat if she knew why the seat was bare. The lady explained:

"All my life I've wanted to come to the Grand Ole Opry," she said. "My husband ordered our tickets over a year ago, but he passed away before we were able to come."

"Oh, I'm so sorry," Johnny replied. "But why did you come by yourself? Why didn't you give the extra ticket to one of your friends and have them come with you?"

"I couldn't," the lady answered. "They're all at his funeral."

CHAPTER EIGHTEEN

I count many of my longtime fans among my close friends. Over the years I've seen them time and time again and gotten to know many of them and their families on a personal basis. There's hardly a stage I can walk on without recognizing several people seated in the audience.

Several years ago I became good friends with two ladies, senior citizens from the upper midwest, who would attend every show I worked within five hundred miles or so of their home. They would follow us even when the bookings stretched out over a period of several days. They'd pack their car and tag right along behind the bus for the entire tour. They would eat in the same restaurants we ate in, check into the same motels, and have seats on the front row of every concert we gave.

We had once been in their area for about a week and were wrapping up our tour on a Sunday with a matinee and an evening performance. Following our Saturday night show, we had driven a couple of hundred miles to the next town and were checking into our motel about two o'clock in the morning.

As I walked through the motel lobby on my way to my room, I spotted the ladies standing by the gift shop, but they didn't see me. I overheard their conversation:

"You want to hit the lounge for a nightcap before we turn in?" one of them asked.

The other one looked at her watch and yawned. "No, I don't think so," she replied. "We'd better get some sleep. We've got two shows tomorrow."

Bluegrass music can be, at times, a contradiction. On the one hand, the genre is known for its rollicking, fun-filled songs like "Rocky Top" and "Roll In My Sweet Baby's Arms." On the other hand, the music is punctuated with sad, mournful songs of lost love and family tragedy—songs like "The Dreadful Snake" and "Don't Make Me Go To Bed And I'll Be Good."

Charlie Collins, longtime member of Roy Acuff's Smoky Mountain Boys, was once asked by a radio interviewer for his description of bluegrass music.

"It's a happy, up-tempo, jazz-type music," Charlie bubbled, momentarily forgetting bluegrass' haunting, dismal melodies of grief and desperation. Remembering quickly, he added: "Till you come to all them dead-mother songs!"

I first got acquainted with most of the fans whom I know personally through the mail. They would write me a letter, I would answer back, they would write me another time or two, and eventually we'd meet at a concert on the road somewhere. I would gradually begin to put a name with a face and pretty soon a fan would become a friend.

I received a tremendous amount of fan mail early in my career, much of it as a result of my weekly syndicated television show which was seen on stations all across the country for nine years. When people care enough to invite you into their homes once a week, they feel they know you almost as a member of the family. I also became known as an artist who personally read his mail and answered it. That, in turn, prompted even more people to write.

Most fan letters a country music artist receives are simply expressions of the writer's appreciation for the artist's music. Some request autographs, some ask for pictures, many seek information on the artist's tour schedule and upcoming record releases. A few get a little more personal.

"If you're ever in (a-town-which-shall-remain-nameless), South Carolina," a very attractive girl once wrote singer Jackie Ward, "stop by Burger King and 'have it your way.'" Enclosed was a picture of the shapely young lass with nothing on but her Burger King hat.

A lady wrote me that she had recently overextended herself a bit financially and wondered if I might make her next month's car payment for her. And a young female fan in Kentucky wrote and said she was moving out of her parents' home and into an apartment of her own, "just in case you ever want to come see me."

Most letters I have received over the years have been extremely nice, but not all of them. And I've never known an artist who couldn't recall a negative letter or a negative comment from a fan quicker than he could a flattering one.

I've gotten letters from people who didn't like the clothes I wore on a particular television show and letters from people who didn't like the way I styled my hair. Negative letters usually have one thing in common—they come unsigned and with no return address. I throw those in the trashcan.

A man once wrote that he had attended a concert of mine and "the music was so loud it hurt my ears. I'll never come back to see you again if you don't turn the music down." I was surprised that he had signed his name.

I wrote him back, apologized for any problems we might have caused, and I asked him where he happened to have been seated at this particular venue. I immediately got a reply.

"I was on the front row," he boasted, "where I could see everything. I was right in front of the speakers!"

I didn't bother writing back and telling him that those speakers were designed to provide sound for several thousand people seated throughout the building. Someone with sensitive ears couldn't have picked a worse place to station themselves. No wonder he thought we were loud!

I never think about stories that have to do with sound systems, though, that I don't recall the night I was standing on stage in a little theater in Virginia, long after our show had ended, shaking hands and signing autographs for the last few fans preparing to leave. I was just about to put my pen away and head for the bus when I saw two ladies charging down the aisle.

They weren't walking, they were running. At least the younger lady was running, grasping the older lady by the arm and virtually dragging her behind as she raced toward me and the spot where I stood.

"Mr. Anderson! Mr. Anderson!" the younger lady shouted. "Don't leave. Please. My mother needs to talk to you!"

Mel Tillis once decided to fire two of his band members, but in an effort to address each musician and each problem individually, Mel thought it best to call the players in to meet with him one at a time.

After he told the first band member he was letting him go and explained why, he said, "Now, g-go get so-and-so and t-t-tell him to come in."

To which the newly-terminated musician replied, "You go get him. I don't work for you anymore."

◆

Little Jimmy Dickens once had a band member quit his job without warning.

"Aren't you even going to give me a notice?" Jimmy asked, puzzled by the player's unexpected actions.

"Yeah," the musician answered disrespectfully, "tomorrow when you look for me, you'll 'notice' I'm gone."

I stopped what I was doing, flashed a smile, and said, "I'm not going any-where. How're y'all doing?" And I reached out my hand.

The younger lady, who wasn't young at all but probably in her mid-to-late fifties, never acknowledged my greeting. Instead she barked, "My mother said to tell you that was the worst show she's ever seen. She says that music was the most awful mess she's ever heard in her life!"

I stopped dead in my tracks. "Really?" I asked, wondering what in the world might have happened to upset the smaller, white-haired woman. All the other fans had been bragging on the show.

"She'll tell you," the daughter replied. "Tell him, Mama." And she nudged the little old lady with her elbow.

Mama didn't say a word but stood staring at me with a puzzled expression that told me nothing. I decided to not wait for her to speak.

I quickly knelt down on the edge of the stage and reached for the elderly lady's hand. I guessed she was probably in her eighties. I looked into her soft white hair and questioning eyes and said as gently as I could, "Honey, what's the matter? Was there something wrong with the sound of our show?"

The little lady's brow never unwrinkled. She stood staring quizzically up at me, saying nothing. Then, all of a sudden, she screamed at the top of her lungs, "*HUH?*"

Immediately I realized the problem. It had nothing to do with our music or our sound system. The little old lady was simply deaf as a post. She hadn't heard anything we had said or done all night. I smiled and gently patted the top of her hand.

"Never mind, sweetheart," I said, smiling and patting, patting and smiling. "Thanks for coming and...and, uh...just you nevv-err mind!"

I have received some wonderful fan mail over the years. I've received let-ters from couples who have fallen in love to my music, gotten married because of my music, and raised their children on my music. I've had fans write and tell me of having had my music played at weddings and on special wedding anniver-saries. I've even been told of fans having had my hymns played at a loved one's funeral.

There have been many tender, touching letters, but there was one I will never forget. It came from a young lady in Canada, and it took me back to a night in the late sixties when I had played a concert in her hometown.

I remembered the night well. Jan Howard was touring with me, and we were booked into an ice hockey arena in eastern Ontario. Prior to the show, we were sitting backstage killing time in the dressing room when a man came by and asked if he might speak with us a moment. We said, sure, and he walked in.

He sat down and began to softly tell us about a young man from the town who, he said, had wanted to attend our concert more than just about anything in the world. All he had talked about for weeks was our coming to town, telling everyone how forward he was looking to seeing our show. But only a few days before we arrived, this young man had been critically injured in a motorcycle accident. And he was lying cut, badly broken, and only semi-conscious in a hospital bed on the other side of town. The prognosis for his survival was not good.

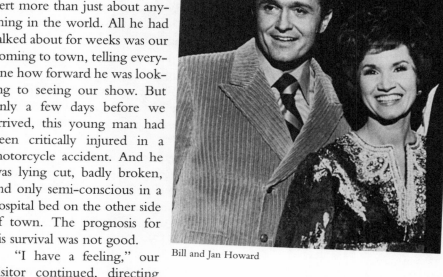

Bill and Jan Howard

"I have a feeling," our visitor continued, directing his request toward me, "that if you and Jan would just take a minute of your time and go by the hospital to see this young man it would be the best medicine anyone could possibly give him. He may not even recognize you, but he'll know you were there. I can't tell you how much he loves and admires both of you. If you'll just go see him, I'll be glad to drive you over and I'll bring you back."

Fortunately, there were two shows set for that night with over an hour's intermission scheduled between the ending of the first show and the beginning of the second. Jan and I agreed we would go to the hospital between shows. "But we've got to come directly back," I cautioned. "We can't afford to be late." The man said he understood fully, and told us he would be in his car with the motor running outside the stage door at the end of the first show.

I was surprised to find when we arrived at the hospital that the "young man" we had been told about was a big, strapping dude, well over six-feet tall and probably weighing over two-hundred pounds. His name was Arthur, and to my further surprise, he was married and the father of several children. I had expected, for some reason, an irresponsible teenager.

Arthur was hurt every bit as badly as our visitor had indicated. I remember seeing legs in casts, arms in casts, wires and tubes connected to virtually every part of his body. He was apparently receiving large doses of medication, and he appeared to be only partially awake.

Jan and I walked over to his bedside and told him who were. We told him we were sorry he had gotten banged up so bad that he couldn't make it to our show. And we told him that we fully expected him to get well so that the next time we were up that way he could come to see us. We tried to keep everything on a light, positive note, but it wasn't easy. The young man was obviously very seriously injured. He could barely move his eyes to let us know that he was even aware we were in the room. I left his side feeling less than hopeful.

But God is still in the miracle business. The next contact I had with him was a letter from the family a few months later telling me that Arthur was improving. And the letter thanked me over and over again for having taken the time to come see him. "You and Jan coming to the hospital gave him the will to live," the letter said. "He says he is going to get well enough to come see your show next time you're here. And we believe he will."

I was back in the area again in about a year, and I thought of Arthur and wondered how he was and how his recovery might be coming along. I didn't have to wait very long for my answer. For when we pulled up to the arena, here came a big, husky guy in a motorized wheel chair grinning from ear to ear. He hugged my neck so hard he nearly broke me in two. All the family hugged me too, saying repeatedly that our visit to his hospital room was the medicine that saved his life.

Bobby Bare

Bobby Bare gives new meaning to the term "laid-back." He rarely gets excited and hates to get dressed up for any occasion. Once during the taping of a television show, he began complaining that he even had to wear make-up.

"Soon as this is over," he said irritably, "I'm gonna go walk through a car wash."

The next time I saw Arthur he was in the parking lot outside my office in Nashville. He had gotten well enough to drive, and with the help of a special apparatus connected to the steering column of his car, he drove nearly a thousand miles to come see us at the Grand Ole Opry. He was truly a living miracle.

I stayed in touch with him and his family over the years. I saw him several more times, and he never failed to mention the visit Jan and I had paid him during the darkest moments of his life. And then I didn't see him or hear from anyone in the family for quite some time. One day I received a letter from his oldest daughter. It was very simple and to the point. She said simply that

Arthur had become very ill and had died. She told me very few details. But she wrote one line that will stay with me forever:

"Thanks to you," she said, "I had a daddy for twenty years."

◆

Nearly every artist I know has received at least one fan letter during his career that was very nice but at the same time was just plain funny. Like the one that came to me back in the late sixties from a lady in California.

She began by saying she was a big, big fan of mine and that she wanted more than anything in the world to move to Nashville to be near me. I don't have the letter anymore, but I read it so many times I almost committed it to memory. It went something like this:

"I will do anything for you when I get to Nashville. I will wash your clothes, baby-sit with your children, cook your food, it doesn't matter. I just have to be close to you.

"I must tell you, however, that I don't have any way to get to Nashville, so you will have to come to California and get me. I live high on a hill, so you'd best come in a helicopter. But don't worry, I will pack light. I will only bring one suitcase and a hat box.

"Please don't laugh at me, Mr. Anderson. I am serious. I love you so much I just have to be near you. Please let me know when you will be here. I want to spend the rest of my life close to you." And she signed her name.

And then, below her name, she wrote one of the classic postscripts of all time:

"P.S. If you can't use me, please give this letter to Johnny Cash."

◆

Connie Smith tells of once receiving a letter from a male admirer who wrote suggestively, "I would love to see you lounging on your couch in a black negligee." Connie admits to having been flattered until she read the next line:

"And there's a green pick-up truck for sale down at Beaman's. I want you to buy it for me."

◆

When I was hosting the game show "Fandango" on the Nashville Network, a lady wrote me a similar type letter. The flattery in the opening lines got my attention:

"Bill, I love 'Fandango,'" she wrote. "It is my favorite show on television and you are my favorite host. I love all your music. You are my favorite singer. You are my favorite songwriter, too." Then she got to the point.

"The reason I am writing you is this:

"Would you introduce me to the Statler Brothers?"

◆

While my wife, Becky, was recovering from life-threatening injuries sustained in an automobile accident in 1984, I occasionally mentioned on stage and in interviews that I was serving as both mother and father to my six-year-old son. A fan asked a band member in all seriousness one night, "How old is Bill's six-year-old son?"

◆

In my capacity as national spokesperson for the PoFolks Restaurant chain, I get to meet many of our guests personally and engage them in conversation. Often I will ask them why they chose to dine at PoFolks.

"I'll tell you why I'm here," one good ol' boy said in answer to my query. I expected to hear that he liked our fried chicken or our catfish. Or maybe our country fried steak with cream gravy lured him in the door. But his blunt answer surprised me:

"I'm here" he said, "cause Western Sizzler pissed me off!"

CHAPTER NINETEEN

When people talk and journalists write of the late fifties, the sixties, and the early seventies in country music, they naturally focus on the men and women who were the major influences of the time.

Names come up like Chet Atkins, Owen Bradley and Billy Sherrill, three of the era's top record producers; Wesley Rose, Jim Denny and Jack Stapp, pioneer music publishers; Hubert Long, Lucky Moeller, and Hal Smith, giants among the first talent agents; Frances Preston of BMI and Jo Walker of the Country Music Association, undeniably the two most powerful women on the early Nashville music scene.

When songwriters are discussed, the conversation usually begins with Harlan Howard, followed by Hank Cochran, Willie Nelson, Mel Tillis, and Roger Miller. Artists? How about Ray Price, Buck Owens, Loretta Lynn, Charley Pride, Tammy Wynette and Merle Haggard for starters, each one a dominant chart-topper every time out.

But, to my thinking, there were other people who contributed much more to our music and to our business than the years have, or probably ever will, give them credit for. Neither is likely to ever be immortalized in country's Hall of Fame, but two good friends of mine, in particular, made large and lasting, although somewhat unheralded, contributions to our music and our art form. They deserve a mention.

One was a major star, a prolific songwriter, and an accomplished musician who has, by choice, all but disappeared from the entertainment scene today. They called him "The Southern Gentleman." His name: Sonny James.

Anybody who has a country music reference book can call forth statistics about the amazing list of consecutive No. 1 record hits Sonny James had—sixteen in a row from 1967 to 1971— but that's only a small view of a much larger picture. What Sonny James did, and has received so little credit for, helped change the face of country music itself.

◆

When people ask me the biggest difference in today's country music compared to the country music I grew up with and first began writing and recording, my answer is always the same: Country music has gone from being a negative music to being a positive music. It's gone from being predominantly sad, mournful, beer-drinking music, full of a whole lot of "you broke my heart, little darlin'" types of songs, to being a music that is unafraid to celebrate the good and the positive things in life. And the man who first precipitated and pioneered the negative-to-positive change on country phonograph records was Sonny James.

Take out a list of Sonny James' consecutive hit records and pick out some titles at random: "My Love," "A World Of Our Own," "True Love's A Blessing," "Born To Be With You," "I'll Never Find Another You." There is a common thread through them all. Each song sings of something "positive" in life, in love, or in a relationship. True, Sonny occasionally sang of unhappy endings— "Empty Arms" and "Only The Lonely," for example—but never once did he promote lyrics of despair, futility, or self-destruction. In contrast to so many country songs of the day, the vast majority of his songs lifted up love and happiness and the good things in life. None dwelled on the sordid or the hopeless.

Positive songs are the very backbone of country music today. In fact, it was when country music began to embrace the more positive songs that its audience began to grow. Younger people began to tune in. A broader base of listeners began to emerge, simply because more people can identify with and relate to positive songs than to negative songs. But the first person to build a career on nothing but songs of this type was not Paul Overstreet nor Michael Martin Murphy nor even Marie Osmond. It was Sonny James.

Sonny James and Bill

For a long time, those of us in the music business weren't aware of just what Sonny was doing nor how he was going about it. We would open up our *Billboard* and *CashBox* magazines every Monday morning and see Sonny either at the top of the charts or on his way to the top with a new record, and we'd scratch our heads and wonder how he kept it happening time and time again.

Blessed now with twenty-twenty hindsight, it's not all that hard to figure. When each new record would come onto the market, it was greeted by full-page ads in the music magazines—*Billboard, CashBox,* and the rest—touting "Another #1

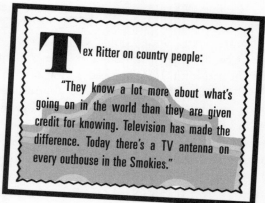

hit from Sonny James," or words to that effect. A few weeks later there would be a follow-up ad: "Sonny James—Well On His Way To Another #1 Record!"

Sonny and his manger, the late Bob Neal, Elvis's first manager, were brilliant. Their tactics were simple: Take one well-crafted, positive song, cut a well-produced, commercial record on it, and then plant the seed in the minds of the disc jockeys and the record-buying public that the record is going to No. 1.

That's exactly where Sonny's records went—sixteen times in a row.

People who read and study about country music in its purest form have been led to believe that today's country songs are an extension of the old folk songs of England, Ireland, and Scotland (which they probably are), and they naturally assume that country music is, and therefore has always been, extremely popular on the other side of the world. That's what I mistakenly thought, too, when I first moved to Nashville.

I came to find, however, that country music as we knew it in this country in the sixties and seventies was virtually unknown at the time outside North America, save for small pockets of hard-core fans sprinkled around the world. The other unsung hero of this chapter helped change that.

On the surface, George Hamilton IV would have seemed an unlikely choice to become country music's Mr. International Ambassador, but with vision, persistence, and a bit of good fortune sprinkled along his path, that's exactly what he became.

George the Fourth came to Nashville not from the farm, as did many country singers of his day, but from middle-class roots in western North Carolina. His father was the first full-time employee of the company that produced Goody's Headache Powders. George Hege Hamilton III eventually rose to the position of vice president and general manager of that company.

George IV was a college student at the University of North Carolina in the late fifties when he cut a song called "A Rose and a Baby Ruth" for Colonial Records, a small local company. The record, which also served to launch the songwriting career of another college student, John D. Loudermilk, was an instant smash hit. It was picked up for national distribution by the much larger ABC-Paramount record label, and almost overnight George became a nationwide singing sensation. Although he had grown up idolizing Ernest Tubb and the stars of the Grand Ole Opry, he suddenly found himself not in country music at all, but rather cast upon the unfamiliar and, for him, ultimately uncomfortable turf of a new field of music called rock 'n' roll.

George's musical roots were undeniably country, though, and when his rock 'n' roll career began to tail off, he headed for Nashville and his original dream of singing on the Grand Ole Opry.

Things started off well for George when he arrived in Music City. He had acquired sufficient name recognition during his brief foray into the pop music field to open the doors at RCA Victor records, and producer Chet Atkins signed him to record country music. He joined the Opry cast, had a million-selling record in 1963 called "Abilene," and was out to conquer the country music world. But just as George—the conservative, well-dressed, well-mannered college kid—had been anything but the typical rock 'n' roller, he was anything but the rhinestone-wearing, honky-tonk, singing country cowboy either. His was more of a button-down, three-piece-suit-and-a-tie image, and that image probably served to hinder his mass acceptance by country audiences in America. Yet it turned out to be the key that opened an even larger door half a world away.

"I had gone to England in '69 for the first country music festival at Wembley," George recalls now, "and had volunteered to go back again in 1970. That's what we did then, we 'volunteered.' There was no money to be made, but something about England and the British country music scene infatuated me. I had stopped in London on my way home from a tour of U.S. military bases in Germany back in '67, and it was love at first sight. I loved the cabs, the architecture, everything."

It was while he was appearing at the second Wembley Festival, sort of a British version of Fan Fair, that George's big break came. The British Broadcasting Company was videotaping the festival for television, and the director Philip Lewis sat before the monitors in the mobile truck outside the building both surprised and intrigued by the British audience's love for and acceptance of country music. This was the heyday of The Beatles, The Rolling Stones, and even Tom Jones, and Lewis was accustomed to a totally different musical environment than what he was finding at Wembley. Not only was the music different, but the audience was different. He liked what he saw and heard. The wheels in the mind began to spin.

As the head of broadcasts that originated outside the studios of the BBC-2

Most people have probably forgotten that it was George Hamilton IV and his fellow North Carolinian, John D. Loudermilk, who started the first sightseeing tours to the stars' homes in Nashville back in the sixties.

They were very successful, so successful, in fact, that larger companies like Gray Lines and even the Grand Ole Opry came along with their own tours and, in effect, put George and John D. out of business.

These tours have spawned many a funny story over the years. I once lived in the same neighborhood as the Everly Brothers, and every tour bus in town came up our little street. I was playing tag with my very young daughter early one morning when she darted out the front door clad only in her panties. I chased her, wearing nothing but my pajama bottoms. Imagine my delight when I looked up and saw forty cameras hanging out a bus window, all pointed in my direction.

"We came by your house on a bus tour when we were in Nashville," a lady once told me at a concert. "You sure do need to cut your grass!"

Another fan once handed me a picture at a road show someplace and, grinning, he asked, "You recognize that?" I looked at the photo and saw a house I had never seen before.

"No, sir, I don't recognize it," I replied. "Should I?"

The man laughed in my face. "What's the matter? You been on tour so long you've forgotten your own house?"

"But that's not my house," I answered.

"Sure it is," he said indignantly. "The tour guide pointed it out to us. Johnny Cash lives next door to you on one side and Faron Young on the other. I've got pictures of their houses, too." He showed me his snapshots, and they were definitely not the homes of Johnny or Faron.

It took me a moment to realize that some unscrupulous tour operator was saving gasoline and misleading the fans by driving into one neighborhood and telling them that a cluster of stars lived in the first group of houses they came to.

Jeannie Seely's bus tour story, however, may just top them all.

She tells of the night she and her songwriter husband, Hank Cochran, had been downtown partying, and without realizing it had consumed a bit more alcohol than they had intended. They were only sober enough to know that neither of them was in any shape to be driving home.

"We were beginning to wonder if we were going to have to spend the night on the sidewalk," Jeannie says, "when we looked up and saw one of the Tours Of The Stars' Homes buses approaching.

"We flagged it down, got on, and when it stopped in front of our house, we got off!"

network, Lewis began to ponder the possibilities of developing a TV series built on country music. But he was questioning whether or not the conservative, staid British televiewer would accept the flash and glitter and down-hominess of the country music artists.

> Country singer George Hamilton IV once met the movie actor, plain ole George Hamilton. The conversation immediately turned to the similarity of their names.
>
> "I had to learn 'Abilene' in self-defense," George the movie star told George the singer. "People were always asking for it at parties. I used to tell them it was your song, not mine. Now I just sing it for 'em."
>
> ◨
>
> George the singer was interested in George the movie star's family lineage. "Are you a Junior or a IIIrd or a IVth?" he asked.
>
> George the movie star replied, "No. My father always told me to make a name for myself, not a number."

"About that time here I came, walking on stage in my pinstripe suit with my button-down collar and my tie," George smiles today, "looking like nobody else on the show and like nothing Philip Lewis associated with country music at all. Supposedly he took one look at me and asked the person seated next to him, 'Who is *that*?' When someone told him my name he said, 'That just may be the guy we could use to bridge the gap between the British public and country music. The cowboys and Indians might be a bit far out, but this guy looks like he would be reasonably palatable.'

"It's funny. The perception of my short hair, my suit and tie, was too citified for the honky-tonk market in this country, but it worked to my favor in Britain. The same image that was too uptown here was perceived as being gentlemanly there. Looking back, I'd say the image is what opened the door."

And what a door it turned out to be. George the Fourth was tapped to host Britain's first country music television series. It began production in the fall of 1970 at a London pub called, appropriately enough, The Nashville Room. George's backing band was a group from Liverpool called The Hillsiders.

"Like everyone else, I associated Liverpool with The Beatles and rock music," George says, "and here came these guys from there playing steel guitars and getting off on Buck Owens' songs and pure, traditional American country music. Young guys, too. Some of them had even gone to school with the Beatles. I couldn't believe it."

George's TV show, titled "George the IV—A King In The Country," was an instant success. After the first two seasons at the Nashville Room, the show began to originate from various locations throughout England, once spending a season taping inside an old palace in Hertfordshire that had been occupied centuries ago by King Henry VIII.

The shows were on the air for seven years, and with their success came offers for George to tour the British isles, to record an album of all British songs with the Hillsiders, and to eventually become the first American country singer to perform in the Eastern Bloc countries. "I was in the right place at the right time," he says modestly. "I fell into it."

He also worked at it. Hard. He travelled to Prague, Czechoslovakia, early in 1974 where he performed for 26,000 people in four concerts. That led to an invitation to visit Moscow later that same year where he starred in a one-man show on the history of country music. Not only did he sing, but through an interpreter, he told the crowds at Moscow University stories about the origins of country music, its role in American culture and beyond, and he played tapes of country singers ranging from the early songs of Gene Autry to the latest hits from Charley Pride.

From there he went to the Railway Workers Institute, where he sang "every train song I could think of—from 'The Wabash Cannonball' to 'Life's Railway To Heaven.'" He was invited to the Palace Of Culture, where he met and interacted with Moscow's leading musicians from all fields of music. "They called it a 'cultural exchange,'" George laughs. "I called it an '*agri*-cultural exchange.'"

George's trip behind the Iron Curtain came six months prior to the more

Promoter Mervyn Conn (second from left) and George Hamilton IV (right) in Red Square.

highly-publicized Soviet tour by Tennessee Ernie Ford and the cast from Opryland. Later tours followed with Roy Clark, the Oak Ridge Boys, and others. "I think they used me as the guinea pig," George says. "When I was there, they were testing the waters to see how country music would be accepted."

In 1982, George recorded an album in Czechoslovakia. In August of '91, he did a television special in Prague, the first country music show under the New World Order.

Today, the admitted number-one project of the Nashville-based Country Music Association is to further the exposure and acceptance of country music beyond the shores of North America. They are making headway. There is now a separate country music chart in the British musical press, whereas in the past, country records were dumped (usually unsuccessfully) into the same charts with pop and rock 'n' roll. More country artists are touring successfully overseas. Some have become major stars. Country Music Television, the all music-video sister station of The Nashville Network, is now available in Europe, and everyone expects the TV exposure available via this service to create even more major stars. The sky seems to be the limit for country music worldwide.

George Hamilton IV was not the first country artist to reach beyond the United States for his success. Slim Whitman, Jim Reeves, Hank Locklin, Johnny Cash—all made their mark overseas prior to George. But George took our music to new places; exposed it, via television, recordings, concerts, and lectures, to new fans in new countries. And, by the very nature of the man himself, he gave it increased class and dignity.

For that we should all be grateful.

CHAPTER TWENTY

The closest friend I have ever had in the music business should not have, by all rights, even been an entertainer. He should have been a professional baseball player. I've got to believe that's what his father had in mind that cold January day in 1936 when he named his newborn son for two of the greatest who ever played the game, Rogers Hornsby and Dizzy Dean.

But Roger Dean Miller didn't know—literally—which end of the bat to hold. He proved that once in a televised celebrity softball game when he stepped up to the plate gripping the bat by its barrel, waving the handle menacingly in the air. I hurried over to the batter's box and showed him how to turn the bat around, even going so far as to take his fingers and wrap them around the small end of the club. I quietly assured him he would have a much better chance of making contact with the ball if he tried to hit it with the big end of the stick.

And, lo and behold, he proved me right. He swung viciously at the first pitch and bounced a hard grounder to second. At the crack of the bat, he leaped out of the batter's box and ran with all his might toward the base. Reaching the base, he slid in ferociously. The ball had not yet arrived. He jumped up quickly, dusted off his uniform, and smiled cockily, only to hear the umpire yell, "You're out!"

Roger had made it to the base, all right, but there was a slight problem. He was standing on *third* base. He had run the wrong way. By the time he realized his mistake, they had thrown him out easily at first.

But he got a big laugh from the crowd and that's all Roger Miller ever wanted anyhow. His hits—and there would be many—would come in a different arena, thank you very much.

With the exception of Sheb Wooley, who was once married to Roger's sister, I knew Roger Miller longer than anyone in the music business. There was a period of time when we were closer than brothers. And I loved him like one. When he died of throat cancer in the fall of 1992, at the far-too-young age of 56, I felt as though a part of me died along with him.

I recounted in my autobiography the story of how we met. Roger was barely out of his teens and in the army, assigned to Special Services at Fort McPherson, Georgia. He sang and played fiddle in a Third Army country music band called The Circle-A Wranglers. I was an eighteen-year-old college student and small-town disc jockey in Athens, some sixty miles away.

We met one Sunday afternoon backstage at a Grand Ole Opry show at the old Tower Theater on Peachtree Street in Atlanta. We swiftly discovered in each other a similar deep affection for country music, along with a true sense of appreciation and respect for a well-written country song. We found we each held a burning desire to be a part of whatever the mystical world of country music was all about. We were both possessed with a drive to be creative—to compose our own songs—and we spent many a Sunday standing alone in the wings behind the stage trying out our latest creations on one another. Every time a show would come to town we were there—watching, listening, absorbing, and longing.

Roger Miller

Roger's chance came first. When he was discharged from the army, he took off for Nashville. He supported himself and his wife, Barbara, by working as a bellhop in the Andrew Jackson Hotel, meeting everyone in the music business he possibly could, biding his time until his big break would come.

It came in rather strange and yet somewhat typical music business fashion. He was in the right place at the right time.

Minnie Pearl was about to embark on a summer-long tour of state and county fairs and was in the process of putting together a back-up band. She had hired another newcomer to Nashville named Mel Tillis, and had told him to be on the lookout for a fiddle player. Mel had met Roger briefly, knew he played a bit of fiddle, and knew he was looking for a job.

> A newspaper reporter once asked Roger in an interview, "Do you have any plans for the movies?"
>
> To which Roger replied, "I sure do. I'm going to see 'Driving Miss Daisy' next week."

It just so happened that Mel went into the coffee shop of the old Clarkston Hotel one afternoon, a favorite hangout for country music pickers and singers in those days due to its close proximity to WSM, and spotted Roger sitting at a table in the back corner. Roger was dressed in his bellhop uniform from the Andrew Jackson.

"Are you s-s-still l-l-looking for a j-j-job?" Mel asked Roger, his stammering and stuttering even more pronounced than now.

"I sure am," Roger replied.

"You wanta p-p-play f-f-fiddle with M-m-m-Minnie Pearl?"

"How much does it pay?"

"Eighteen d-d-dollars a day."

"I'll take it!" Roger said excitedly. "But wait here. I've gotta go back over to the Andrew Jackson and give my two minutes notice!"

◆

I could fill an entire book with Roger Miller stories. He said more funny things and did more funny things—more crazy, off-the-wall things—than just about anybody who ever lived. Based on his sense of humor and his approach to life, it would be easy to think of him as a buffoon, an overgrown child, but nothing could be farther from the truth. Roger Miller was the closest thing to a genius I have ever known.

In spite of his limited education (he finished only the eighth grade) he had a command of the English language that the most learned scholars would envy. He played with words like they were his own personal toys:

"I've Got Half a Mind to Leave You—But Only Half the Heart to Go."

"The Last Word in Lonesome Is Me."

"If the wolf had ever come to our front door, he'd have had to brought a picnic lunch." All Roger Miller originals.

I've never told many people, but that line from my signature song, "Po' Folks," was a Roger Miller throwaway. He was bemoaning his own financial condition one day and the words just rolled off his tongue. I cracked up.

"That's a great line for a song," I exclaimed.

"It'll be another 'Poor Little John,'" he laughed, poking fun at an obscure song from early in his career.

When I wrote "Po' Folks" I tried to give him credit, but he wouldn't take it. According to Buddy Killen, who published Roger's songs, that was typical.

"Every songwriter in town used to follow Roger around," he says, "just to pick up his 'droppings.'"

◆

Anyone who was ever around him for any length of time can recite a Roger Millerism or two. Some of my favorites include:

"The state flower of Tennessee is Martha White."

"I once knew a guy who lied so much he had to get someone else to call his dogs."

"I caught him in the truth one time, but he lied his way out of it."

"When I was a little boy, I wanted to grow up to be a gravel pit. Actually, I wanted to be a comedian, but everybody laughed at me."

"I once was so hot as a songwriter that I wrote a letter home and it got up to No. 8 in the charts!"

"I was so hot I had to get an unlisted driveway!"

"If I ever make any money in this business, first thing I'm gonna do is go home and pave the farm."

"Things are so slow for me the buzzards are circling my career."

"I once dreamed that I died, and my whole life passed in front of my eyes. Trouble is, I wasn't in it."

And, looking out into the first gleam of daylight after one of his many all-night escapades: "Uh-oh! Here comes God with His brights on!"

Overheard backstage at the Opry House during the taping of the television special honoring the life and career of Minnie Pearl:

"I've never seen so many stars in one place at one time in my life. If a bomb were to fall on this building tonight, tomorrow morning Soupy Sales would be the biggest act in country music!"

— Actor David Huddleston

◆

Glen Campbell to Pee Wee King as Pee Wee sang his signature song: "How could you have been dancin' to the 'Tennessee Waltz' when it hadn't been written yet?"

◆

George Lindsey, who portrayed "Goober" on the "Andy Griffith Show," to nobody in particular as the taping ran far into the night: "By the time we get finished with this, Opie will be eighty years old!"

Roger had been in Nashville for more than a year when a few good things started happening for me. He took almost as much joy from my successes as I had from his.

He was the first person to call and tell me that Ray Price had recorded my song, "City Lights," which turned out to be the break I needed to get a toe-hold in the music business. He introduced me to Buddy Killen, nudging Buddy to sign me as a songwriter. He recommended me to some of the first promoters who ever booked me on the road. And he once lent me the last twenty-five dollars he had to his name.

We had returned to Nashville from a long and highly unsuccessful tour stone broke. I wanted to go home to Georgia and re-think this whole music business career, but I didn't have enough money for a plane ticket. My car was in such bad shape I didn't trust it to make the journey.

Roger wasn't a whole lot better off than I was. He and Barbara were down to twenty-five dollars in a joint savings account. But he insisted, over both Barbara's and my objections, that I take it and fly home. Reluctantly, I agreed, but I promised that as soon as the plane landed in Atlanta I would go directly to Western Union and wire the money back to him. I knew there was a small royalty check from "City Lights" waiting at my parents' house.

Dad met me at the airport, my check in hand. I was so overwhelmed by what Roger had done—lending me his last twenty-five dollars—that when I reached the telegraph office, I wired him back thirty dollars.

The next morning Roger called at the crack of dawn, sobbing into the telephone. He thanked me over and over for being so generous. I told him it was no more than what he had done for me, and I tried to hang up. But he kept right on thanking me and crying about what a great guy I was. By the time I finally managed to get him off the phone, he had spent more money thanking me than the five extra dollars I had sent him in the first place.

I will never think of Roger Miller but what I'll remember the night not long after I had moved to Nashville when he phoned me in my little cabin to see what I was doing. I told him I was getting my dirty clothes gathered for a trip to the wishy-washy.

"I've got a bunch of dirty clothes, too," he said, "and I hate going to the coin laundry. Why don't I bring my clothes over and we'll go together?" I knew he and Barbara couldn't afford a washing machine, and I was glad to have the company. In about an hour he pulled into my drive.

At the time, he was driving the smallest car I had ever seen. It was a tiny, midget Fiat of some kind, about the size of a riding lawnmower, and it looked like a toy. Roger called it his "popcorn Fiat" and boasted constantly about his good gas mileage.

I squeezed my lanky frame into the only passenger seat and tossed my bag of dirty clothes into a tiny opening between the back of the seat and the rear window. We set out for the coin laundry. On the way, Roger kept complaining about how much he hated having to do his washing. I admitted that I wasn't overly fond of the exercise myself, and I added, "If Mama was here I'd get her to wash these clothes for us."

Roger perked up. "Where is she?" he asked.

"In Atlanta, I guess. Why?"

"How far is it to Atlanta?"

"About 250 miles," I replied. I could hear the wheels in his mind begin to roll faster than the wheels on the Fiat.

"Hey, if you'll put the gas in the car I'll drive us to Atlanta," Roger exclaimed. "And we won't have to go to the damned-ole wishy-washy!"

"How much will that cost?" I asked, laughing at the absurdity of his suggestion. Two-hundred and fifty miles to wash clothes? I really didn't think he was serious. Even if he was, I figured it would be out of my price range.

"Well, I get about sixty miles to the gallon in this thing," he answered. "I know a place out on Murfreesboro Road where gasoline is about twenty cents a gallon. We can go down to Atlanta and back for less than two dollars. Hell, time we wash and dry all these clothes at the coin laundry, we'll have spent more than that!" And he roared with laughter.

To this day, my mother still shakes her head and laughs in disbelief at the picture in her mind of her only son and his wacko friend clutching two sacks full of dirty clothes, standing on her front porch ringing the doorbell at midnight.

"What are you doing here?" she asked, glad to see me but totally puzzled.

"We need to get some clothes washed," I said, laughing hysterically at the thought of our having driven six hours from Nashville to Atlanta to get out of spending one hour at the coin laundry.

And my mom, super lady that she is, laughed right along with us. Then she proceeded to stay up till the wee hours washing and drying clothes for a couple of wanna-be country music stars. Roger and I did our part by quietly falling down across the twin beds in my old bedroom and going sound asleep.

◆

My mom and dad came to love Roger Miller almost like an extra son. In later years when he reached superstardom, he never forgot their love and caring. They saw him in concert several times in various cities across America; never once did he fail to welcome them warmly and treat them special.

Dad's favorite remembrance of Roger, however, was not at a concert but at the hospital in Nashville when my oldest daughter, Terri, was born. Dad spent most of the weekend standing outside the nursery peering in through the glass at his first grandchild. Every time Roger would come by, there was Dad in the same spot, just staring. Finally, Roger walked up, put his arm around Dad's shoulder and asked, "What are you trying to do, Mr. Anderson, memorize that baby?"

◆

It's a wonder my folks ever spoke to Roger again after the stunt he and my sister, Mary, pulled on them a few years later.

The Andersons and the Millers had decided to get away from Nashville on a little vacation together. Seven of us left Music City in two cars headed for beautiful Jekyll Island on the Georgia seacoast—me, my wife, and Terri; Roger, Barbara, their son, Alan, and their newborn daughter, Rhonda. By the time our little caravan reached Atlanta, however, Roger and Barbara had decided bringing baby Rhonda along had been a big mistake.

She was too young, they said, and needed too much attention. The Millers grew fearful that their much-needed vacation was about to turn into anything but a vacation.

I don't remember just whose idea it was, but someone came up with the solution: Leave Rhonda in Atlanta with my parents for a few days. We could hit the beach with the older kids, relax and have some fun, then pick Rhonda up on our way back to Nashville. Surely my parents would love having a six-week-old baby in the house again. How long had it been anyhow? Our only problem was, we couldn't find them to tell them how much fun we were going to let them have. We searched everywhere we knew in Atlanta, but my folks were nowhere to be found.

We didn't have a lot of extra time to kill, so we drove to my sister's house. At the time, Mary resided in an orbit almost as far above the earth as Roger's, and she said Rhonda would be welcome to stay with her until our parents surfaced. In fact, she and Roger gleefully plotted a little surprise for them when they returned.

I wasn't there to see it for myself, but the story is legendary in our family. It seems that when Mom and Dad got home and walked up onto their front porch, they discovered a basket had been left there for them. Their first thought was that it was a basket of flowers, or perhaps fruit, brought by a thoughtful friend. Upon closer observation, however, they realized the basket contained a blanket with a note pinned to it. It was only when they bent down to read the note that they heard the faint cry of a baby.

"Dear Mom and Dad," the note read. *"My name is Ursula. I am the German war orphan you ordered."*

By the time they got over the shock and Mary confessed to having left Roger's newborn baby on the doorstep, Roger was two hundred miles away without a care in the world—pulling on a bathing suit over his skinny frame and saying, "My legs always swell up this time of year."

◆

Where do the stories stop? I could tell them forever.

I was at Roger's house the morning he drove his black '49 Ford into downtown Nashville only to return home at sundown on a riding lawnmower. I watched as he swung the bright orange mower into his yard and cut a two-foot-wide path through the knee-high grass all the way from the street up to his front steps. Then he jumped off the seat with the gleeful shriek of a child and turned off the engine, never to touch his shiny, new plaything again.

"We can't afford a riding lawnmower," Barbara cried as she ran down the steps and into the yard.

"It only cost eleven dollars," Roger laughed.

"You can't buy a riding mower for eleven dollars," she chided.

"But that's all it cost," he insisted, winking at me and softly adding, "Down."

◆

In 1989, Roger got stopped for speeding.

"Where are you going in such a hurry?" asked the policeman who pulled him over.

"I'm late for Red Foley's funeral," Roger said seriously.

"Oh," said the policeman, "well take it easy." And he tore up the ticket.

Roger was late for Red's funeral all right. Red died in 1968.

◆

In 1970, Roger had just opened his first King Of The Road hotel in Nashville. He was thrilled beyond words when he called and invited me to join him for dinner and to tour the facility. I congratulated him, accepted his invitation, and told him I was excited about something new in my life as well.

"I want you to meet my new lady," I said. "Her name is Becky, and if you don't talk her out of it, I think she might marry me before long." I told him Becky and I would meet him in the lobby of his hotel the following Saturday night at six.

Becky had only recently moved to Nashville, and was supporting herself at the time by working in the political campaign of a man named John Jay Hooker, Jr., who was running for governor. She had heard me speak of Roger Miller ever since we had met, and she was anxious to meet him, but there was a slight problem. Mr. Hooker would be needing her to attend a big political rally that Saturday afternoon. She couldn't possibly get away to join Roger and me until after six o'clock.

I told her that rather than alter Roger's plans, I would go on down to the King Of The Road by myself at six o'clock and she could join us there as soon as the rally was over.

About 6:30, Roger and I were sitting in the lobby of his beautiful hotel catching one another up on the news. Suddenly I looked up and saw Becky trying to work her way across the crowded room. But she was having a tough time. It seemed as though every man in the room was trying to engage her in conversation as she walked by. Finally she reached my side and I immediately recognized the problem. In her haste to leave the political rally and come to the hotel, she had neglected to remove her campaign ribbon—a bright yellow ribbon pinned to her dark blue dress proudly proclaiming, "Hooker." That's all it said. Not "Vote for Hooker" or "John Jay Hooker." It simply said "Hooker."

Before I could explain or introduce Becky to Roger, he looked at her and said, "Boy, Nashville sure has changed since I lived here. It used to be against the law. And now they advertise!"

◆

The last time Roger and I worked a concert date together he came to my bus between shows and we ate dinner. We laughed and relived the old times. Country music had changed a lot since our old days together backstage at the Tower Theater. And, we admitted, we had probably changed a bit ourselves.

"You know what we are, Anderson?" he asked between bites of steak and baked potato.

"Yeah," I replied. "Dinosaurs."

"No we're not," Roger said in a rare serious moment. "We're survivors."

◆

As we visited, a lithesome, long-legged blonde in an extra-tight pair of light green shorts walked in front of the bus. She didn't exactly "walk," she slithered—her already-too-small shorts creeping farther and farther up into her natural crevices with every step.

Roger sized it up. "She's flossing," he said.

The last time I saw Roger Miller was at the taping of the "Tribute To Minnie Pearl" television show in May, 1992, six months before he died.

I knew of his recent bout with throat cancer, but like everybody else in Nashville, I was under the impression that the cancer was in remission and he soon would be as good as new again. He stopped me in the hallway backstage and we talked.

"Have you got a good doctor?" I asked him.

"The best," Roger answered. "Doctor Ossoff."

But he couldn't be serious for long. "I think his first name is Frazier" he said. "No wonder his office is so cold. His name is Frazier Ossoff!"

As I went to leave the Opry House following the show, I saw him again. A night of performing and visiting with old friends had taken its toll on his already weakened vocal chords. He could barely speak. He pulled on my coat sleeve.

"Hey, Anderson," he whispered. "I'm stealing your act!"

I laughed.

But I might not have laughed so hard had I realized those would be the last words I would ever hear from a very dear and cherished friend.

CHAPTER TWENTY ONE

Owen Bradley, the legendary record producer, arrived at a recording session of mine late one afternoon wearing an uncustomary coat and tie and the look of a man emotionally drained.

He wearily plopped down into his control room chair, loosened his tie, and turned to me, twenty-two years his junior.

"Bill," he said slowly, "you'll know you're getting old one day when you find yourself going to more funerals than weddings." He had just come from the funeral of a friend.

I didn't fully understand his prophecy then, but I never forgot it. Only now have I lived long enough to know how right he was.

I've been going to far too many funerals lately. Or, if not funerals in the literal sense of the word, then memorial services or "celebrations of life" for special people who have passed away.

That's what they held for Roger Miller inside the hallowed halls of the Ryman Auditorium—a memorial service. Hundreds of his friends, associates, and fans gathered, not to mourn his death, but to celebrate his life and all he had meant to each of us. We told Roger Miller stories and we listened to his music and we remembered and we laughed. Roger would have wanted it that way. It was only when no one was looking that we took out our handkerchiefs and rubbed our eyes.

Barely more than six months later, we came together again, this time very unexpectedly. Another friend, Harold Jenkins, known to the world as Conway Twitty, from all outward appearances a young and vibrant fifty-nine years old, had died while on tour in Missouri.

Conway Twitty (R) with Bill (L) and Conway's longtime business manager Hugh Carden.

His memorial service fell during the week of Fan Fair, and the beautiful, modern Baptist church next to Twitty City in Hendersonville overflowed with stars and fans alike. We listened to unreleased cuts from Conway's last recording sessions, to songs and eulogies from people like Ralph Emery, George Jones, The Statlers, The Oak Ridge Boys, Tammy Wynette, Porter Wagoner and Conway's daughters, Joni and Kathy. The service ended with the playing of Conway's "Why Me, Lord?" We listened and collectively wondered the same thing.

There were no flowers at the Roger Miller memorial service and few at Conway's. Roger's family had requested in lieu of flowers that donations be made in his name to cancer research. Conway's family requested contributions in his name to the youth baseball programs that Conway so strongly supported in Hendersonville.

Roy Acuff didn't want flowers when he passed away either. Nor did he want a sad, tear-filled funeral service. He told the members of his family and the hierarchy at the Grand Ole Opry two years before his death to "bury me before anybody even knows I'm dead." He said he had received enough flowers and glowing tributes during his lifetime. He didn't want his friends to feel like they had to give him anything else when he was gone.

They adhered to his wishes. He died at 2 a.m., November 23, 1992, and even though the news of his death began leaking out about daybreak, he was resting in Spring Hill Cemetery by ten o'clock that morning.

◆

Mr. Roy was a very special man, and I feel fortunate to have gotten to know him in a very special way. He and I became duet partners in the late seventies on a song called "I Wonder If God Likes Country Music," and as a result, I got to see a side of him that not everyone was privileged to see. When he died, I felt I lost not only a hero but a very good friend. And yet the first time he and I ever appeared together on the Opry, it was a near disaster.

Roy hadn't been in Nashville much during my earliest days in the music business. He was on a major tour of Australia, then when the tour ended, he stayed Down Under and filmed a series of television shows. Consequently, even as I began to get acquainted with most of the Opry stars and they began to know who I was, I remained a stranger to Roy Acuff.

He hadn't been back in the States very long when I was assigned one Saturday night to appear on his segment of the Opry. I'm sure he saw the name Bill Anderson on his program and wondered, "Who in blazes is that?" Someone must have pointed me out to him, however, because just before I was set to go on, he came over to where I was standing backstage.

"Are you Bill Anderson?" he asked loudly, attempting to talk above the music being played on stage.

"Yes, sir," I answered, and I reached to shake his hand. I didn't feel a whole lot of warmth in return.

"What label do you record for?" he hurriedly asked.

"Decca," I replied.

"What?" he shouted. The music was drowning me out.

"Decca," I said again, trying hard to be heard above the din. "Decca Records."

"Never heard of it," he answered coldly.

Roy Acuff was mowing the lawn at his home one day when a lady driving a big Cadillac pulled over to the curb and let her window down.

"Young man," she called out, not recognizing Mr. Roy, "how much do you get for mowing a lawn?"

Sizing up the situation quickly, The King of Country music playfully called back, "The lady I mow this lawn for lets me sleep with her!"

The driver quickly raised her window and sped away.

> Opry star Del Reeves remembers his earliest days in the music business as having been extremely lean.

"It was my first long tour," he recalls, "and me and another guy in the band were literally starving to death. We were down to thirty cents between us. We were both new on the job and scared to ask the bandleader for an advance.

"Finally, in desperation, we went to a little grocery store and bought two boxes of Jell-O. We ate the powder right out of the box, then we each drank a big glass of water. The Jell-O swelled up in our stomachs and kept us from feeling hungry 'til we got paid.

"I guess I wanted to be in this business awfully bad!"

I knew better, and I moved to correct him. "Yes, sir, you have," I said. "You used to record for them yourself. Decca Records. DECCA!"

About that time the song on stage ended and Mr. Roy turned and walked back out into the spotlight.

"Here's a young man I've never heard of before," he announced coolly to the crowd. "Never heard of the company he records for, either. It's called Jacob Records. But make welcome Mr. Bill Anderson."

Jacob Records? Had I been so intimidated by meeting "The King Of Country Music" that I actually blurted out something that sounded like *Jacob* Records?

I don't recall what I sang that night, but whatever it was I'm sure I did a lousy job on it. All I could think of standing center-stage at the Ryman Auditorium was Roy Acuff thinking I recorded for some company called Jacob Records.

◈

I had been a Roy Acuff fan for as long as I could remember. How could anybody be a country music fan in those days and not be a fan of Roy Acuff's? It would have been virtually impossible.

I lost count of all the Roy Acuff records I had in my collection as a youngster. I had "Wreck on the Highway" and "Pins and Needles (In My Heart)" and "The Great Speckled Bird" and goodness knows how many others. When I became a disc jockey, I had access to hundreds more. And I played them many times on my radio programs.

The one I got the most requests for was new in those days, but it's classic now, a Dusty Owens song called "Once More."

I saw Roy Acuff in concert long before I ever moved to Nashville, and was quite taken by the fact that he was so generous in featuring the various members of his band on stage. He allowed each of them their moment in the spotlight. He appeared to not have the inflated ego of many stars. I later learned that entertaining the audience was Mr. Roy's sole concern. He didn't care who got the glory so long as the paying customers got their money's worth. To my way of thinking, that's a big part of the reason he was a superstar right up to the end.

◆

A Nashville music publisher and longtime friend, Chuck Chellman, sent me the song, "I Wonder If God Likes Country Music." I liked it the very first time I listened to the demo tape, but it wasn't exactly the kind of song that was burning up the charts in the late seventies.

And yet there was something very haunting about both the storyline and the melody. I couldn't get it out of my mind. I took the demo on the bus and played it for the band. They liked it as much as I did and encouraged me to record it. When I began selecting songs for my upcoming album, I played it for my producer, Buddy Killen. It was then that I realized something was missing.

The demonstration recording had been sung in its entirety by one person. "What that song needs," I said to Buddy as we listened to the tape, "is somebody to play the part of the old man. There needs to be another voice on the record."

Buddy agreed. "Do you have anybody in mind?" he asked.

"Somebody who sounds like Roy Acuff," I said. And I mentioned a singer I knew in Kentucky named Esco Hankins.

"Why don't you just get Roy Acuff himself?" Buddy asked.

"Oh, he wouldn't do it," I said. "Would he?"

"He won't if you don't ask him."

"Gee, I don't know . . . . I'm not sure if I . . . ."

"You want me to call him?"

I was glad to lay the project in Buddy's lap. "Would you? That would be great! He might do it for *you*!" I was ecstatic.

Buddy was unable to reach Mr. Roy right away, but we went ahead and cut the musical tracks to the song on my next session anyhow. I laid down a scratch vocal track on the verses to give anyone who heard it a rough idea of how the song was to be sung. But when it came time for the vocal on the choruses, I left the track blank.

I had to leave town and go on tour the next day. When I returned, Buddy summoned me to the studio.

"Take a listen to this," he smiled. And the engineer turned on the tape machine.

When the song reached the chorus and Roy Acuff's penetrating voice came blaring from the mammoth control room speakers, chill bumps raced across every inch of my body. I wanted to cry and scream "Hallelujah!" at the same time.

"How did you get him to do it?" I asked, overwhelmed by the sound of my voice on the same tape with Roy Acuff's.

"I just asked him. He was tickled that we wanted him," Buddy replied.

"Recording companies aren't exactly beating down his door right now, you know. He really seemed to enjoy doing it."

◈

I honestly don't remember the first time Mr. Roy and I sang the song on stage, but I know I was nervous. I had thanked him profusely for making the record with me as soon as I saw him following the session, and he had been extremely gracious. He seemed to be, as Buddy had indicated, very pleased that we had wanted him.

I began to notice a difference in his attitude toward me not long afterward. It wasn't that he had ever been unfriendly, it was just that he and I had never seemed to have much common ground between us before. And now all of a sudden people were coming up to each of us and saying how much they liked our record and asking us to perform it on the Opry. And Roy's mail began to be filled with compliments and requests for the song from his fans.

I don't recall his ever coming to me and asking to do the song on stage. It was always the other way around. I would go to him. And there was a ritual I would always follow.

About an hour before my Opry spot, I would ease over to his dressing room. I would sit down with him and begin to talk about baseball or something in the news that I knew he was interested in. We would grow relaxed together, and finally I would pop the question.

"You want to sing our song tonight?"

His answer seldom varied. "You really want me to?" he would ask, a slight tone of uncertainty in his voice.

"Sure I do," I would say.

Then he would ask if he might come over to my dressing room first and rehearse with the band. I didn't realize in the beginning, but the King of Country Music was a bit unsure of himself. The song was new to him, and it had been years since he had learned a new song. Plus, he wasn't used to singing with me or my band. The rehearsals seemed to relax him.

I have never minded rehearsing. In his case, I welcomed the opportunity to be around him more, to understand him better. I came to realize that in spite of all his natural ability and commercial success, he could be insecure in uncharted waters. I was surprised at first, but I know now it was just one more thing that went into making Roy Acuff the consummate professional.

◈

I knew Mr. Roy and I had become friends the night I asked him to do the song and he replied, "I don't know why you want me to sing with you."

"Because you're Roy Acuff," I answered. "You're the King of Country

Music!"

"I know," he laughed, "and I'll steal the show from you, too!"

I assured him that was exactly what I wanted him to do.

◆

By the late eighties, MCA Records no longer had in their catalog the album containing "I Wonder If God Likes Country Music." Roy and I were still singing the song on the Opry and on television shows together, fans were still requesting it and wanting to purchase it, but the recording was unavailable. I decided to take the situation into my own hands.

I went into the studio with my band and recorded my part of the song again. By this time, Mr. Roy was approaching eighty-five years of age and was growing too weak to travel to a recording studio and spend several hours standing before a microphone. So when it came time for him to do his part, I tried to make things as easy for him as I could.

He had a ritual he followed nearly every day. He would leave his home at Opryland around noon and walk over to the Opry House. He would drink a cup of coffee, collect his mail, visit with Opry manager Hal Durham and the Opry staff—relaxing for a couple of hours before returning home. Hal said he thought this would be a perfect time for Roy to ease into the control room backstage and sing along with the new musical tracks we had laid down.

It worked perfectly. We had everything set when Mr. Roy entered the room. He sang the chorus of the song two times, cracked a couple of jokes off-mike, and went back to his daily routine. The whole exercise didn't take fifteen minutes and we had a crisp new version of a song that was on its way to becoming a country classic.

◆

Now that we had the new recording, I wanted more than anything to film a video on the song. I felt the storyline would lend itself to a marvelous production, and I was right.

Keith Durham, a former coal miner from southwest Virginia, now an audio engineer for the Nashville Network:

"The worst day in the music business is better than the best day in the coal mines."

◆

Before going to work for TNN, Keith was my sound engineer. Once on a tour through the Pacific northwest, I noticed his wrist watch was two hours faster than mine, which I had set to local time. He had a simple but heartfelt explanation:

"It took me thirty years to get to where I could set my watch on Nashville time. I'm not about to change it now!"

Again, I wanted to make the experience of filming the video as unobtrusive for Mr. Roy as possible. I went to him and explained what I wanted to do, and asked if he would like to take part. He hemmed and hawed a bit and said something about not knowing why I needed him, but I could sense that deep down he was again pleased that he had been asked.

To make the filming as easy as possible for him, we decided to shoot his part of the video at the Opry House, with a limousine to drive him to his closing scene downtown at the Ryman. And again we worked around his schedule.

About nine o'clock in the morning we set up the lights and the cameras and began to film the scenes in which Mr. Roy would not be involved. When he arrived at his normal time around noon, all he had to do was walk out and perform.

The director, Stan Moore, was wonderful. He patiently explained to Mr. Roy that the character in the song wore cowboy clothes that were "frayed and worn" and asked him if he would mind changing from his customary white shirt and tie into a costume more fitting. Mr. Roy, who had never in his career chosen to wear the gaudy western attire of many country singers, smiled and cheerfully put on a bolo tie and cowboy boots.

He may have been in his late eighties, but when the lights came up and the camera began to roll, Roy Acuff had the spirit of a twenty-year-old. He did everything Stan Moore asked of him. Not only did he wear the unfamiliar western clothes, but he held and pretended to play a flat-top guitar. Roy was a fiddle player. So far as I know, he had never played a guitar in his life.

◆

Because the story of "I Wonder If God Likes Country Music" revolves around an old man picking up my guitar and singing a song to my band, I invited the members of my Po' Folks Band to appear in the video along with me and Mr. Roy. They were thrilled at the opportunity to be seen on camera with a legend.

At the time, I had a very attractive young lady in my group named Marcia Wells. In one scene, she was seated close to Mr. Roy. I noticed that every chance he got, Mr. Roy would look in Marcia's direction and smile. I teased him about it.

"I thought you said you were having trouble with your eyesight, Mr. Roy," I said. "How come you're always looking at Marcia?"

He smiled. "I may have trouble seeing *some* things," he shot back, "but I can *always* see a pretty girl!"

> **T**ennessee Ernie Ford said his father gave him the best advice he ever received regarding show business: "He always told me, 'Don't ever get any bigger than the person who buys the ticket to see you.'"
> The Ol' Pea Picker never did.

CHAPTER TWENTY TWO

T here's a last time for everything.

For me and Roy Acuff, it came on a Saturday night in mid–October, less than six weeks before he died.

It was the weekend of the Grand Ole Opry's sixty-seventh birthday celebration, and the eighty-nine-year-old Mr. Roy had been taken to the hospital. The doctors wanted to keep him overnight and run some tests. He was exhausted and needed rest. Fluid was building up around his heart. The last place The King of Country Music needed to be that night was on stage performing.

The Opry schedule, however, had been made out in mid-week, and as always, Mr. Roy was scheduled to host the eight o'clock portion of the show. I was slated to be one of his guests. But shortly after 7:30, Hal Durham came into my dressing room and asked if I would headline the show instead. "They want to keep Roy at Baptist overnight," he said calmly. I agreed and quickly ran through a couple of extra songs with the band.

About two minutes before eight, I was standing in the wings waiting for the big red curtain to come down on the previous Opry segment when I heard a rustling of bodies and a murmuring of voices off to my left. I could scarcely believe my eyes when I looked up and saw Roy Acuff—weak, feeble, his eyesight failing him, his steps slow and unsure—leaning on the arms of his band members and being led gently to the stage. He was dressed impeccably as always—a light-colored sport coat, white shirt, bright tie. There was no doubt but what The King intended to perform. A giant collective gasp went up among the several hundred cast members and Opry visitors backstage. None of us could fathom this pale, frail man doing what he seemed so determined to do. I held my breath.

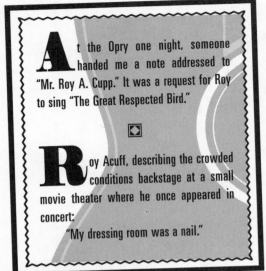

At the Opry one night, someone handed me a note addressed to "Mr. Roy A. Cupp." It was a request for Roy to sing "The Great Respected Bird."

Roy Acuff, describing the crowded conditions backstage at a small movie theater where he once appeared in concert:

"My dressing room was a nail."

But he did it. The curtain went up, the Smoky Mountain Boys hit the musical train-whistle intro to the "Wabash Cannonball," and Roy Acuff's voice filled the night just as it had on Saturday nights for over fifty years:

"From the Great Atlantic Ocean
To the wide Pacific shore . . . ."

I stood in the shadows and watched in amazement, fearful of what might happen, and yet in total awe of this simple mountain man who had achieved worldwide acclaim, a legend who had dined with presidents and kings but who never felt quite as comfortable, never quite as at home, never quite as happy anywhere in the world as he was on stage at his beloved Grand Ole Opry.

Roy finished his song, made a few brief, sometimes barely audible remarks, and paused for a commercial announcement. Somebody whispered to him that I was to be his first guest.

When the commercial was over, Roy leaned against a stool and made a few kind remarks about me—how I was from Georgia and was a big baseball fan and was pulling for the Braves to win the World Series—and introduced me to the crowd. I smiled, waved to the audience as I made my way to center stage, and then impulsively did something I don't recall ever having done before in my life. I changed my mind and decided I wanted to sing a totally different song from any of the ones I had rehearsed with the band.

"Mr. Roy, I want you to sing a song with me," I said.

He looked surprised and said something about it being my spot and why didn't I just sing one of my songs.

"Because I want to do a song with you," I protested. I was shocked at the words coming out of my mouth. I had never sprung the song on him as a surprise before. I couldn't believe I was doing it now.

In a moment the audience joined in my pleading—clapping and urging him to sing with me—and Mr. Roy leaned back against his stool and reluctantly gave in. I signaled my guitar player to kick off "I Wonder If God Likes Country Music."

From the very first notes of the song, I knew. We had sung this song together dozens—maybe even hundreds—of times. We had recorded it twice, filmed it as a music video, performed it on Roy's Fiftieth Anniversary TV Special on NBC, sung it on "Hee-Haw," and performed it countless times on the Opry. But I knew. Never before had it felt like this.

It was all I could do to tell the story—the narrative of an aging, broken-down musician who never quite made it in the music business. In the lyric the old man is bemoaning the fact that his quest for stardom cost him his wife, his family, and what little money he might have accumulated along the way. He admits his voice is cracked now, his dream is gone, and yet he confesses sadly, "pickin' and singin' is the only life I know."

At that point, the song changes from my telling the story of the pitiful old man to Roy Acuff actually assuming the man's character. By this time, the old man knows his life has been a failure and his only hope for fulfillment lies in the hereafter. Roy prayerfully sings the old man's despondency:

> *I wonder if God likes country music.*
> *Will there be a place up there to sing my song?*
> *Will He make my fingers nimble like they used to be,*
> *So I can play the chords and sing along?*

There's never been a man who could sell a song to an audience quite like Roy Acuff. When we first began performing this song on the Opry, Roy would stay off stage during my part, letting me paint the picture and set the scene by myself. And then, just as the old man in the song began to ponder his fate, Roy would step out into the spotlight, his white hair shining like a halo, and begin to sing.

When he would reach the line about God making the old man's fingers "nimble like they used to be," Roy would pause and look down at his own aging hands and move his fingers ever so slightly. The audience would be in a trance.

But this time it was different. During my part of the song Roy never left center stage. He propped his weary body against the padded seat of the stool behind me and held his wireless microphone limply in one hand. When it came time for him to sing, he weakly took only a couple of steps forward and leaned against the base of an unused microphone stand.

He never even opened his eyes. He stood facing more toward me than toward the audience—the wireless mike in one hand, the other hand clutching the mike stand in much the same way an anxious child might wrap his fingers around the leg of a loved one he fears might go away. But he never missed a note. Never missed a beat. He never missed a word.

I stood but a few feet away—watching, marvelling, totally absorbed—when I began to feel the moisture slowly creeping into the corners of my eyes. The tears came gradually at first, clouding my vision, trickling one at a time down

Roy Acuff performing with Bill for the last time.

my cheek. And then when Mr. Roy came to the line about God making his fingers nimble and I realized he couldn't even muster the strength to open his eyes and look at his own fingers, the dam gave away completely. I stood there in front of 4,400 hundred people and a radio audience of countless millions and cried like a baby.

I'll confess. I had wondered on previous occasions when we were on stage singing together, "Is this the last time? How will I know the last time when it comes? *Will* I know?" And every time that thought would attempt to invade my mind, I would quickly push it aside and say to myself, "Hey, enjoy this moment. Don't worry about tomorrow or next time. You are the luckiest man in the world. How many people can say they ever sang with Roy Acuff?"

Not very many.

◆

When the song ended I wiped my eyes and walked over to where Mr. Roy was still clinging to the microphone stand. Before I could even reach his side, every person in the Opry House was on his feet applauding. Not just clapping, but cheering and whistling, and wiping tears from off their own faces. Behind me I could hear the sniffles of the band, the announcers, the visitors seated on stage. There wasn't a dry eye in the house.

When I reached Mr. Roy's side, I held out my right arm and wrapped it gently around his aging shoulders. Through the padding in his sport coat I could feel how frightfully thin his arms had become. I squeezed him gently, afraid to apply much pressure for fear I might cause him pain. I leaned over into his expressionless, almost colorless face and I whispered, "I love you."

He did not respond at all. I didn't expect him to, but I know he had heard me. I just hoped somehow he knew how proud I was at that very moment to be there, standing by his side. Me—the kid who used to sit by the window of his bedroom down in Georgia on Saturday nights years ago and twist and turn the aerial on his tiny Arvin radio in hopes of picking up the Grand Ole Opry and hearing Roy Acuff sing through the static.

Me—the kid who used to save his allowance and whatever money he made mowing lawns and delivering newspapers and sacking groceries so he could go to the store on Saturday afternoon and buy a Roy Acuff phonograph record. Or go to the picture show and see Roy Acuff starring in "Night Train To Memphis."

And now, for one last time, the kid stood next to the King. How proud he was.

◇

The crowd continued to stand and applaud. I knew Mr. Roy wasn't able to see out into the audience so I leaned down again and I told him, "They're standing up, Mr. Roy. The whole crowd is standing up."

He still maintained his sense of humor. "They're not going home, are they?" he asked.

◇

This would be the last time we would ever perform together and I knew it. And I accepted it, not because I was glad to see it end, but because I could celebrate the fact that it ever happened in the first place.

And at that moment I knew beyond the shadow of a doubt the answer to the question:

Yes, Mr. Roy, God most assuredly *does* like country music.

He gave us you, didn't He?

EPILOGUE

Most of the country music stars who performed on radio shows back in the forties and fifties developed little catch phrases they would use to bid their listeners adieu at the end of every broadcast. Some of the signature sign-off lines became almost as famous as the stars themselves.

Hank Williams, for instance, would always preface his closing remarks by promising he'd see the folks again, "If the Good Lord's willin' and the creek don't rise."

Hank Snow would say to his audience, "Good luck, good health, and may the Good Lord always be proud of you."

Ernest Tubb's closing line was a slice of country philosophy: "Be better to your neighbors," the Texas Troubadour promised, "and you'll have better neighbors."

Hawkshaw Hawkins carried it a step farther. His parting remark was always, "Don't say anything to your enemies you don't want your friends to know."

Listeners knew the Duke of Paducah was at the end of his comedy routine when he would announce, "I'm headin' for the wagon, boys, these shoes are killin' me!"

And Ferlin Husky, although I never heard him say this on the radio, had two pet phrases he would use to close out every concert I ever saw him perform. After having spent his last few minutes on stage portraying the comedic Simon Crum, he would turn serious.

"If any of you haven't enjoyed the show tonight," he would say in Ferlin's deepest, most sincere tones, "you're welcome to ask for your money back." And then as Simon: "You ain't gonna git it, but you're welcome to ask for it!"

And then, when the laughter had subsided, Ferlin would say in all seriousness, "If we have said anything or done anything to offend any of you here tonight, we apologize. It was due to our ignorance." Pause. "But if you go away mad at us, then you're just as ignorant as we are!"

◆

I've never had a set way of closing out my shows anywhere except at the Opry. When my segment there is finished, I always try to acknowledge the other entertainers who have been on the show with me, the musicians, the background singers, and the announcer who has delivered the commercials from the side of the stage. Then I turn to the audience, hit a chord on my guitar and say, "Til next time, this is ol' Whisperin' Bill saying 'thank you' . . . and leaving you with this." And I sing:

"I Love Those Bright Lights and Country Music."

And you know what? Every time I sing that line, I mean it. Because after all these years, all the miles, all the songs . . . I still love this business and I still love country music.

I don't plan to ever stop.

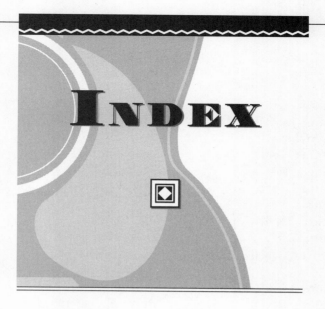

INDEX

C

Call, "Cactus" Jack 87
Campbell, Archie 19
Campbell, Glen 146
Carden, Hugh 154
Carnall, Stu 59
Carter, Anita 33, 57
Carter, Helen 33, 57
Carter, June 57, 62
Carter, Mama Maybelle 33, 57, 62
Cash, Johnny 17, 55, 57, 60-63, 133, 139, 142
Chellman, Chuck 157
Choate, Terry 54
Clark, Roy 3, 45, 142
Clark, Steve 53
Clement, Jack ix, xi
Cline, Patsy 84-86, 89, 91-92, 95, 97-100, 107
Cochran, Hank 17, 65, 135, 139
Cole, Nat King 95
Collins, Charlie 128
Conn, Mervyn 141
Cooper, Stoney 111
Cooper, Wilma Lee 111
Copas, Cowboy 84-86, 89, 91, 94-96, 105, 120
Copas, Kathy 86
Crutchfield, Jerry 88
Crutchfield, Patsy 88
Cutrer, T. Tommy 88
Cyrus, Billy Ray 56

D

Davis, Jimmie 14
Day, Lazy Jim 96-97
Denny, Jim 135
Dexter, Al 9
Dickens, Jimmy 17, 35, 93, 109-110, 129
Dill, Danny 51
Dodd, Ken 71
Domino, Fats 8
Douglas, Mike 10-11
Drusky, Roy 67, 84-86
Durham, Hal 159, 161
Durham, Keith 159

E

Ellis, "Uncle" Len 107
Emery, Ralph 17, 94, 103, 154

F

Felts, Narvel 39
Flatt, Lester 103
Foley, Red 17, 23, 150
Ford, Tennessee Ernie 160
Fox, Curly 101
Franks, Tillman 55
Frizzell, Lefty 17

G

Garrish, Sonny 73-75
Gateley, Jimmy 22, 39, 69, 103
Genova, Charlie 43-47
Gibson, Don 17
Glaser, Tompall 113-114
Graham, Billy 52
Grant, Marshall 57
Greene, Jack 39

H

Haggard, Merle 18, 34, 135
Hall, Tom T. 2, 17
Hamilton, George 140
Hamilton, George, IV 137-142
Hamilton, George Hege, III 137
Hankins, Esco 157
Harper, Laurie 73
Harper, Lisa 73
Hawkins, Hawkshaw 30, 60, 88-89, 91, 93-94, 167
Haynes, Dick 58
Helms, Don 89, 91, 105
Hobbs, Becky 5
Holly, Buddy 107
Homer & Jethro 119
Hooker, John Jay 151
Howard, Harlan 17, 28, 65, 135
Howard, Jan 32, 39, 41, 62, 130-132
Huddleston, David 146
Hughes, Randy 86, 89-91
Husky, Ferlin 17, 32, 81, 167

J

Jackson, Alan 82
Jackson, Stonewall 29
Jackson, Wanda 24
James, Sonny 30, 135-137
Jim, Cracker 34-35
Johnson, Ernest Tubb 118-120
Johnson, Jack 70
Jones, George 82, 154
Jones, Grandpa 33, 96, 110-112, 121

K

Killen, Buddy 1, 54, 66, 147, 157-158
King, Pee Wee 146
Kruger, Jeffrey 71

L

Lance, Jimmy 10
Lewis, Philip 138, 140
Lindsay, Dave 55
Lindsay, George "Goober" 112, 146
Locklin, Hank 142
Long, Hubert 97, 135
Lord, Bobby 63-64
Loudermilk, John D. 10, 17, 138-139
Lynn, Loretta 17, 67, 96, 123, 135

M

Mandrell, Barbara 7
Manual, Dean 103
McBride, Martina 33
McCall, Darrell 95
McClinton, O.B. 122
McCoy, Clyde 64
McDill, Bob xii
McEntire, Reba 101
McGee, Sam 42
Miller, Alan 149
Miller, Barbara 144, 147, 149-150
Miller, Rhonda 149
Miller, Roger 1, 17, 19, 29, 50,
    65, 68, 88, 135, 143-53
Miller, Shirley 83
Miller, Snuffy 52, 62
Miller, Zell 82-83
Moeller, Lucky 135
Monroe, Bill 38, 98
Moody, Clyde 38
Moore, Stan 160
Myrick, Weldon 10

N

Neal, Bob 137
Nelson, Willie 17, 135
Newman, Jimmy C. 29
Nixon, Richard 41

O

Owen, Jim 99

Owens, Buck 40-42, 135, 140
Owens, Dusty 156

P

Parton, Dolly 5, 122
Pearl, Minnie 6, 40, 94, 144-146,
    152
Perkins, Luther 57, 62
Pierce, Webb 17, 37
Preston, Frances 135
Price, James 26
Price, Kenny 39
Price, Ray 3, 17, 135, 147
Pride, Charley 37, 55, 70, 135,
    141
Putman, Curly 28

R

Rainwater, Cedric 90
Rainwater, Marvin 50
Reeves, Del 156
Reeves, "Gentleman" Jim 17,
    101-107, 142
Rich, Buddy 10
Riley, Jeannie C. 79
Ritter, Tex 54, 66, 122, 137
Robbins, Marty 17, 29-30
Robertson, Jim 9
Robin, Don 94
Rodgers, Carrie 60
Rodgers, Jimmie 60
Rose, Wesley 135
Ruby, Texas 101
Russell, Johnny 55, 125